Personal
Financial Planning
in Banks

Personal Financial Planning in Banks

A Handbook for Decision Making

Jeffrey L. Seglin
Jeffrey R. Lauterbach

Bankers Publishing Company • Boston

Library of Congress Cataloging-in-Publication Data

Seglin, Jeffrey L., 1956–
  Personal financial planning in banks.

  Bibliography: p.
  Includes index.
  1. Banks and banking — United States — Customer services
— Handbooks, manuals, etc. 2. Finance, Personal — United
States — Handbooks, manuals, etc. 3. Investment
advisers — Legal status, laws, etc. — United States.
I. Lauterbach, Jeffrey R. II. Title.
HG1616.C87S44 1986   332.1'7   85-28738
ISBN 0-87267-059-7

Managing Editor: Nancy Long Coleman
Cover design: William Samatis

To Robert N. Veres, Editor, *Financial Planning* magazine
Without his input, this book would not be complete.

About the Authors

Jeffrey L. Seglin is a writer and editor whose articles have appeared in *Inc., Venture, Boston, TV Guide, Financial Planning, Philadelphia, Goodlife, Banker & Tradesman, Personal Investing, Enter,* and other publications. He is a contributing editor to *Financial Planning* magazine, as well as the personal finance writer for *Boston* magazine.

He was the content editor for Public Broadcasting System's "On The Money" national television series and serves as a consulting editor to Random House's Professional Publishing Group for whom he developed the *Journal of Financial Services Marketing.*

Seglin is the author of *Selling Ice Cubes To Eskimos, America's New Breed of Entrepreneur: Their Marketing Ideas Innovations & Successes,* (Acropolis) as well as two other Bankers Publishing Company books, *Bank Letter Writing Handbook* and *Job Descriptions in Banking.*

Jeffrey R. Lauterbach is an associate editor for *Financial Planning,* special assignments editor for *Business Atlanta,* and contributing editor for *Restaurant Hospitality.* His articles have appeared in *The Washington Post, Industry Week, The National Law Journal, Sylvia Porter's Personal Finance Magazine, Ohio Business,* and *Atlanta.*

Lauterbach has spoken on financial planning to the AICPA Personal Financial Planning Conferences and other professional groups. He has been a consultant to financial services companies and companies servicing the financial services industry.

Contents

Preface   *xiii*

Chapter 1   What Is Financial Planning?   1

Financial Planning   3
The Financial Planning Process   3
    The six steps of financial planning   *3*
Commitment & Expertise   5
Fitting Financial Planning To A Bank's Operations   6

Chapter 2   Identifying the Market   9

Market Segmentation   11
    What the market is   *12*
    Attracting upscale customers   *13*
    Measuring the potential market — the 10% of 20% rule   *14*
Market Receptivity   14
    Prior relationships   *17*
    What the market wants   *20*
Competition & Deregulation   20
Overall Strategic Plan Mesh   21
Services & Fees   21

Chapter 3   Setting Up Shop — Inside or Out?   27

Mandates for Success   29
Preliminary Decisions   30

Internal Programs   31
Joint Ventures   35
    What to expect of a joint venture   *36*
    Structuring a joint venture   *37*
    Using the joint venture to move in-house   *38*
Conclusion   39

Chapter 4   **Competition in Financial Planning**   **43**

Expansion of Financial Planning Services   45
Competent Advice & Increasing Competition   46
Insurance Companies   47
CPAs   48
Brokers   51
    NYSE firms   *51*
    National Association of Securities Dealers firms   *53*
Independent Planners   54
Major Banks   56
Conclusion   64

Chapter 5   **The Legal and Regulatory Matrix**   **67**

Financial Planning Boundaries   69
Investment Advisors Act of 1940   70
Glass-Steagall Act of 1933   71
Legal Precedent   75
In-House Planning   76
Joint Ventures   79
    National banks   *81*
    State non-member banks   *83*
    Savings and loan associations   *85*
    Federal Reserve member banks   *88*
Rental Agreements   89
Investment and Related Products   94
    Insurance sales   *94*
    Variable annuity contracts   *96*
    Mutual fund management   *97*
    Limited partnership sales   *98*
Conclusion   103

Chapter 6   Securities Law   105

The Complexity of Compliance   107
The Legal Foundation of Securities Regulations   107
The SEC — Chief Among Regulators   108
  Components of an investment advisor   108
  Registration as investment advisor   110
  Recordkeeping requirements   111
State Regulations   116
Broker-Dealer Registration   121
Liability Issues   123
  Exercising reasonable care   125
Conclusion   127

Appendix I   Personal Financial Planning Software   131

Appendix II   Discount Brokers Offering Services To Banks   137

Appendix III   Correspondent Banks Offering Discount Brokerage Services To Other Banks   147

Appendix IV   Market Research Firms   159

Appendix V   Colleges & Universities Affiliated With The Certified Financial Planner (CFP) Program   169

Appendix VI   Case Studies   177

Case Study 1   First Interstate & Pennington Bass   179
Case Study 2   Setting Up An Internal Program At The Savings Bank of Utica   182
Case Study 3   State Bank of Medford, Wisconsin — Innovative Bank-Based Financial Planning   184

Case Study 4   Successful Bank/Financial Planning Firm
            Joint Ventures: Missouri Savings — P&W Ltd.   186
Case Study 5   Larry Carroll & The Bank of Hartsville,
            South Carolina: A Living Partnership   187
Case Study 6   Competition from The Big Eight Accounting
            Firms   188
Case Study 7   Competition from Smaller National &
            Larger Regional Accounting Firms   190

Bibliography   195
Index   201

Preface

Undoubtedly the most talked-about service in the financial services industry today is financial planning. It is the subject of major market advertising campaigns, the rationale behind at least 20 different locally-produced television programs and state regulatory and legislative initiatives from Maryland to Hawaii. Banks and securities firms in Australia, Italy, Canada, and the United Kingdom are all studying the best way to offer the service.

In its purest sense, financial planning represents a new kind of relationship between a financial services company and its clients, a consumer-driven marketing approach in a traditionally sales-driven investment industry. According to recent studies, a majority of households are interested in having a financial plan, and the level of interest tends to go up dramatically with education and income level. While sales professionals measure their time with a client in terms of weeks or months, financial planners seek to build life-long relationships. The planning approach thrives on the recent advent of investment "overchoice" and the complexity of the U.S. Tax Code. Consumers, particularly the more affluent, have become exposed to a new array of investment options. Their portfolios are increasingly multidimensional, designed to minimize current and future taxes, to maximize investment return and liquidity, to meet specific retirement goals and ultimately transfer an estate past the gamut of probate and inheritance taxes. As this process becomes even more complex, financial consumers are learning the value of receiving impartial advice on all aspects of their financial lives from a single professional source.

Because the financial planning service provider looks into every aspect of a client's financial needs, the service he or she provides also crosses the traditional lines of the separate financial services disciplines. A client requires specific advice on tax planning — traditionally an accounting function — as well as the kind of detailed investment planning expertise that is normally associated with a stock brokerage firm. Planners deal with risk management issues that fall into the historical purview of insurance specialists; they offer the kind of trust and estate planning services that are offered by attorneys and the nation's larger banks.

The institution that is prepared to offer these financial planning services in a single package is positioned for the future of the financial services industry. The reverse may also be true. As deregulation proceeds, both in the Congress and through skillful exploitation of legal loopholes, the financial services firm that cannot offer a comprehensive service to its customers could find itself at a fatal disadvantage.

From the perspective of a lending institution, the rapid growth of cross-industry financial services represents perhaps the greatest danger, as well as the greatest opportunity, to come along in many years. The danger comes from competitors — not just banks, but the large, diversified financial services firms as well — who are committing unheard of sums of money to bring their own versions of the financial planning service into the market. Brokerage houses and insurance firms are offering planning because the services can attract customers who were not traditionally interested in working with their representatives. Many of their new customers are your current customers. Through central asset accounts, margin accounts, and insurance policy loans, these firms can now offer many of the same services that your bank does. They are also attracted to the service because financial planning helps them prepare for that forseeable day when banks, brokerage houses, and insurance companies are all providing essentially the same products and services.

The opportunity for lending institutions lies in a virtually unlimited market. Because financial planning emphasizes the consumer's welfare, it is compatible with the service-oriented corporate culture of banks and savings and loan associations. It is, in short, a way for them to enter the lucrative securities industry without sacrificing the close non-sales-oriented client relationship that they have traditionally maintained.

The rules of the financial planning game offer banks and savings and loan associations some formidable advantages over their competitors. Some are obvious: banks have a visible, local presence that tends to reinforce the personal nature of the planning service. They are accessible. They already do business with many of the high-net-worth prospects whose attention other firms spend millions of dollars trying to attract. Most importantly, the lending institution has an image in the public mind of stability, impartiality, and professionalism in a world of "product pushers." Given their choice, many customers would look first to the place where they have established a banking relationship, as long as the company's expertise appeared to be on a par with outside vendors. Since the financial planning process tends to confer some measure of control over the client's entire financial position — much more than the checking and trust accounts traditionally held by depository institutions — it is possible that the more aggressive companies could seize market share from brokerage and insurance firms through a well-conceived approach to the planning service.

This trend is not likely to change in the future. In fact, some of the most cogent observers of financial services deregulation predict that by as early as the middle of the next decade, most financial services and investment products will be offered or sold in the context of a financial plan.

This book was not written to offer any philosophical discussions of why this should be so, or any new ideas about the trends that shape the future. It was written because executives at "grass roots" lending institutions are discovering the need to learn about the planning service and — unfortunately — because, until now, they have had no reliable, practical guidebook to answer their most basic and important questions.

This book was designed to be used as a practical tool, a handbook for the banking executive who is actively considering the various options by which to offer financial planning-related services to his or her best customers. You may be a CEO looking for ways to generate new sources of fee income, a trust officer looking for ways to bring better organization to your increasingly complex customer service menu, or a young executive who has been given the task of finding out how to implement this new financial planning service. In each case, you want to know exactly what the process will entail, what rules and regulations govern the service, how to evaluate and market it, and who in the market can help your institution move from planning to implementation most effectively and economically.

We hope this book will help save capital and human costs. When financial planning capabilities are implemented, this book will serve as a guide to the many service providers who specialize in working with lending and other financial institutions in the same general field.

There are an estimated 30,000 reputable financial planners practicing in every large and small market in the U.S. Many of them would be receptive to joint venture negotiations. They are joined each year by several hundred new prospective planning employees who are earning degrees from a growing number of collegiate programs around the country.

For you, the issue is not "Can I provide the financial planning service?" but rather, "How do we want to structure the service to meet the needs of our clients?" "How much control do we want over the finished product?" And perhaps most importantly, "In what form is financial planning appropriate for our customers, our company, and our employees?"

As you consider these important questions when reading the chapters that follow, we hope you will find more than just the information you need to offer a competitive and quality-oriented financial planning service. We hope that financial planning will allow you, as it has others, to enhance the services you offer to your customers, and to expand your reach in the increasingly complex and competitive financial services marketplace.

Much time and energy has gone into the writing of *Personal Financial Planning in Banks*. The professionals who are mentioned either in the text or the appendixes went out of their way to let us know what they were up to — how they were paving the way to make the road a little smoother for others who followed.

Bob Roen and Nancy Long Coleman of Bankers Publishing Company were committed to the project from the outset. Their editorial insight and input helped to shape and create what finally became the finished book.

Tony Smith, director of financial planning at Kidder Peabody in Atlanta, laid the groundwork for the chapters on regulation. The lengthy file which he compiled and shared with us, as well as his input, are appreciated.

We are grateful to Jack Lange, Editor-In-Chief of *Financial Planning* magazine, whose commitment to publishing a quality magazine is clearly reflected in every month's issue. We acknowledge him both for his encouragement and for giving us the room to learn as we wrote for *Financial Planning*. We value him as an editor and a friend.

What Is Financial Planning?

The financial consumer of tomorrow marches up to the local automated bank teller and requests a broad range of financial services. He may have to step inside to a window. But at one place or the other, he would be able to purchase stocks and bonds, insurance and real estate and conduct traditional banking transactions as well. And if that consumer arrives home forgetting the one household item he set out to buy, he may use his personal computer and order a toaster from the bank's consumer goods subsidary.

Former Treasury Secretary
Donald T. Regan
Testifying before the
House Banking Subcommittee

Financial Planning

Before you can answer the question "What is financial planning?", you really have to answer several questions, all of them crucial to the development of any meaningful business plan in the area of financial planning. From a procedural standpoint, what does the financial planning service involve? What kind of promises and commitments are implied to the clients? From a marketing standpoint, how will the financial planning service help my lending institution in its competition with others in my market? And perhaps most importantly: Can financial planning help capture client assets? Improve my relationship with my lending institution's best customers? Help cross-sell other products and services? Build new sources of fee income?

Defining financial planning is complicated by the fact that it is offered by many different types of professionals who all seem to define it a bit differently. The common denominator is that the planner analyzes the financial resources of a client on an individualized basis to help that client attain certain financial objectives. This will include, but is not limited to, analyses of the client's income, cash flow and liquidity, investment mix, risk management needs and coverage, tax situation, and such subjective issues as retirement goals, short-term needs, risk tolerance, and investment sophistication.

The Financial Planning Process

From a procedural standpoint, financial planning can be defined best by the separate commitments it entails.

The Six Steps of Financial Planning

The industry's largest trade organization, The International Association for Financial Planning (IAFP), defines the financial planning service according to a six-step process. These include:

1. *Collecting and assessing a client's relevant financial data.* This should include not only the client's assets, insurance policies, asset performance and so on, but also the client's investment

risk tolerance as well as his or her current and future tax situation.

2. *Identifying financial goals and objectives*. Does the client want to retire at age 50? Are there children whose higher educational needs will have to be met in a specified number of years? Does the spouse dream of owning a certain home or of taking an expensive vacation? Under various inflation scenarios, how much reserve capital will the couple need at retirement age to enjoy a comfortable income?

3. *Identifying financial problems*. There are often potential tax problems that develop in working with higher net worth financial planning clients, whose appropriate solutions may involve "soft" shelters such as retirement plans or trusts, or through investment shelters, such as tax-exempt municipal bonds, variable life insurance policies, private placement or public limited partnerships

   There may also be a problem with unrealistic expectations, or a wide discrepancy between projected net worth levels and the amount of reserve capital needed for retirement. Returns may not be high enough to justify the expectations that clients bring to the financial planner; a lowering of expectations may be in order or an adjustment in the level of risk that the client is willing to take.

4. *Providing written recommendations and alternative solutions*. This may range from a 200-page plan complete with boilerplate text explaining the various investment alternatives and some detail about the nature of each investment, to brief bulleted recommendations for action. From an ethics standpoint, a key word here is "alternative." Since there is seldom *one* perfect path for an investor to take, it is important that the consumer be given options to choose from, and that the financial planner not take full responsibility for the course of action unless this relationship is specified in writing.

5. *Coordinating the implementation of recommendations*. To many planners, coordination implies direct sales of investment products, either personally or through an affiliated broker-dealer. This is a permissible alternative for lending in-

stitutions and could become a significant profit center. Implementation could also be handled by outside experts. A number of planners, particularly those whose income is derived entirely from fees, prefer to contact an insurance professional to find the most cost-effective risk management policies, a stockbroker to make equities investments, an accountant to handle the tax planning, and a lawyer or banking officer to handle the details of trust establishment and management.

You should not overlook implied questions of ethics. Generally, when a financial planner who also sells investment products creates a plan on a fee basis, he or she does so expecting to follow through on it. When a fee is charged for creating the plan, however, it should be made clear to clients that they are free to go elsewhere for implementation.

6. *Providing periodic reviews and updates.* In an investment environment where the tax laws change significantly every two years, the inflation and interest rates move dramatically, and such far-reaching financial events as inheritances, birth of children, salary increases or unplanned expenses are commonplace, *no* financial plan — even those projecting out five, ten years or more — is really valid for more than a year at a time. By monitoring progress, the planner lets the client know where he or she stands, and also helps build the close, long-term relationship that marks the strength of the financial planning approach in the marketplace.

Commitment and Expertise

In addition to the six steps, financial planning implies a certain level of experience on the part of the provider. Although no planner can be an expert in every financial services field, he or she should be conversant in tax law, investments and their analysis, risk management, estate planning and probate, trusts, and other investment-related legal vehicles.

There are currently a number of recognized educational designations that imply at least passing acquaintance with these areas.

These include the CPA, JD, MBA degree, CFP (Certified Financial Planner), and the ChFC (Chartered Financial Consultant).

Financial planning also implies a certain commitment to the financial consumer. Since this is the key to financial planning's strength in the marketplace, it is overlooked at the would-be planner's peril.

Financial planning represents a significant break from the tradition of the sales-oriented stockbroker and insurance agent. One respected practitioner in the market has compared a financial planner who is more interested in sales than the client's best interests to a doctor who receives a kickback every time he prescribes medicine. Some planners, in fact, maintain that investment products cannot be recommended or sold on a commission basis under such a relationship since it implies a divided loyalty on the part of the seller/planner. Others prefer to maintain close control over the client's investments and use the commission to ameliorate the often high cost of investment analysis.

Bank-related financial planners fall into both camps, and into a third camp as well: selling banking services, where appropriate, in the context of a financial plan, yet being compensated on a salary basis.

As with any professional consultation, the financial planning service also implies a strict adherence to confidentiality. Many would-be clients are not accessing financial planning services currently because they are reluctant to make public the details of their financial situation. The planner who violates this confidence is unlikely to regain it.

Fitting Financial Planning to a Bank's Operations

From an operational standpoint, financial planning represents a strong organizational principle. Because it relates to all aspects of a client's financial life, the service can easily become the center of reference for your company's traditional and non-traditional products and services. Money market accounts become the repositories of the liquid assets portion of your client's portfolio. Your IRA and Keogh-related services could handle the client's retirement accounts. The discount brokerage operation could handle the plan "implementation" — the actual purchase of investment products — more cheaply and easily than many service providers in the market today.

The service could also become a structure on which the bank or savings and loan association could hang new customer services and ventures that would have previously fit uncertainly or not at all into the company's corporate structure.

From a marketing standpoint, financial planning represents a two-edged marketing opportunity. On the one hand, the market for comprehensive investment analysis and planning services is still largely untapped. Research indicates that anywhere from 30 percent to 50 percent of all families in the U.S. are interested in receiving comprehensive assistance with their financial lives. Fewer than 10 percent have ever done so. Fully 70 percent to 75 percent of the "affluent market" — those with $50,000 incomes and above — recognize the need for financial planning. Fewer than half have ever received a financial plan. Still fewer have an ongoing planning relationship.

For the lending institution, this offers an opportunity to offer a needed service and to build a closer relationship with an increasing number of customers. Marketing the service should increase traffic. At best, it could lead to a steady expansion of market share.

On the other hand, financial planning capabilities represent a chance to cross-sell the discount brokerage services, money market accounts, IRA and Keogh-related services that represent largely untapped income sources at many smaller lending institutions. Once a planning relationship is established, extending credit can become an easier and more convenient process for the customer, as well as a more secure one because the lending officer is intimately familiar with his or her financial condition. The customer is, in effect, pre-approved.

From an operational standpoint, the financial planning service has the often-overlooked virtue of flexibility. Throughout this book, we offer a number of similar, but not identical definitions of the financial planning service, where the global, consumer-oriented approach to financial services has been translated into different corporate cultures. It is a profit center at one bank, a loss leader at another. It is a customer service, a tool for cross-selling, an organizing principle, a means of positioning the lending institution of today to enter the financial services market of tomorrow.

The basic structures that currently appear in the marketplace require varying degrees of involvement by the staff of the lending institution. Some companies are offering the service in-house, run by members of the staff either through the trust department or a private banking department. They are either hiring outside planners on a salary basis, adding in-house training programs or funding the further education of staffers designated as future planners, or they are contracting with a computer analysis firm to perform the actual numbers analysis and print out the financial plan. In the latter case, bank or savings and loan employees collect the raw data from the client and offer a counseling service when they present the finished plan.

Other financial institutions are entering into joint venture arrangements with outside service providers. These may be local planning firms who set up a branch office on the bank's premises, or "turnkey" financial planning firms who jointly employ the depository institution's personnel and supply the back office services on a private label basis. Or they may involve the establishment of a separate entity, capitalized by the bank and staffed by an experienced planner, which accesses the bank's list of customers or is advertised through the bank's marketing campaign. Still others are simply offering referrals, on the theory that helping a customer manage his or her assets is going to be better for the client relationship in the long run.

Even if the basic outlines remain relatively well defined by the market at large, the financial planning service is flexible enough to accommodate the many diverse needs of an industry in the throes of transition. The question of what financial planning is can be answered generically in terms of opportunity, of qualifications, and of implied commitments to the customer. The finer details of financial planning services must be answered by you and others in your office, based on your needs and how best the service can work for your company and its customers.

2

Identifying the Market

If bankers are looking at financial planning as a product which will be profitable and which will help position the bank and the trust department for long-term growth and profits then it is an important opportunity.

Dr. Philip D. White
Associate Professor, Marketing
University of Colorado, Boulder
Addressing 1985 ABA National Trust & Financial Services Conference

Market Segmentation

In business and banking circles today, there appears to be a growing concern with an elusive "middle market" that must be captured in order to succeed in the marketplace. Financial planning and banking are no exceptions. The middle market is now the major focus for both of these industries.

But this "middle market" that everybody wants to capture is a slippery category. What should bankers look for as they move into financial planning in the years ahead? How can they identify the prime candidates for financial planning services among their current and prospective customers?

It's important to have a firm understanding of your potential marketplace before you embark on a new venture like financial planning. Just who is the market you're trying to capture? The research is certainly available. We hope that by distilling the volumes of research, you may come away with a sense of who your bank's financial planning customer could or should be.

Many small banks are moving into financial planning to serve the affluent, sophisticated client who, on the average, makes a good income, has money to invest, and knows that it is prudent to plan. This market signifies a hefty number of potential financial planning customers. Recent studies put the number of households with incomes above $40,000 a year at above 15 million. Those with incomes between $40,000 and $70,000 are the prime candidates for the financial planning services offered by banks or other practitioners.

Richard P. Austin, vice president of marketing for First Financial Planner Services, a firm that has nationally launched a package of financial planning support services to banks, points to the fact that bankers' appetites are being whetted by the results of recent marketing studies that show that families with incomes of $40,000 and up would consider using bank financial planning.

James Shanahan, director of new product development at Chemical Bank, points out that Chemical's surveys agree with Austin's perceptions: planning is appealing to customers under 55 who earn between $50,000 to $70,000 a year.

The results of a focus group study performed by Chemical Bank paint an interesting picture of market segmentation for financial planning services. (See table 2.1 on page 16.)

Some surveys, however, show the average income level for prospective financial planner users significantly lower than the Chemical Bank mark. Market Facts, Inc., a Chicago-based market research firm, concluded in their December 1983 survey that the "average customer" for bank financial planning services met the following profile:

Average age: 40.7 years

Income: $28,400

Occupation: Professional or Manager (32%)

Education: At least some college

Family Size: 2.9 persons

"That profile implies a relatively young, well-educated prospect in the family-raising years," the Market Facts report stated.

Market Facts also recognized additional markets that had not been clearly identified before. "There is clearly a *second* market consisting of older, less well-educated families out of the child-raising years," the study relates, "and a *third* market of much younger families, many without children or with very young children." The common denominator among all three segments is their need for financial planning services that could help them build a solid financial base on which to plan for the future.

James B. Fox III, president of First Interstate Bankcorp's Investment Service Company, paints a picture of a potential market that not only matches the consensus of what others looking at the field conclude, but also brushes broader strokes of what the market is and what it needs: "Wealthy individuals need more than traditional investment management or a package of bank services," he says, "they need the broad-based guidance of financial planning."

It is the sophisticated investor the banker must try to attract to the bank's financial planning services. The income level of this "middle market," upscale, or affluent customer may start somewhere between $40,000 and $70,000 a year, but how else can the potential market for bank financial planning services be identified?

What the Market Is

The results of a poll conducted for Infoware Corporation of Nashville, Tennessee, about households interested in personal financial planning, gives some insight into the potential market for financial planning services. In the spring of 1985, the company found that around 70 percent of households interested in financial planning would consider changing their current financial institutions to one that offered the service.

Infoware's poll also found that those most likely to use financial planning were young families, with members under 30 years of age; pre-retirees, 50 to 59 years of age; and affluent individuals with annual incomes of $40,000 or more. Only 11 percent of those surveyed were familiar with what financial planning actually was, but 65 percent of them had heard of it. The study concluded that interested individuals will be more inclined to use financial planning as they gain a stronger familiarity and understanding of it.

The Infoware study presents no startling revelations, but it offers clear confirmation that people — particularly upscale customers — want financial planning services. More importantly, they are willing to shop around to find a financial institution that will offer them. The banker who counts on customer loyalty for continued profits must now cope with the fact that 70 percent of the households surveyed in this poll would be willing to change institutions to find the financial planning services they desire. In this light, developing financial planning services may soon become a necessity for survival, rather than the optional offering some lending institutions now perceive it to be.

Attracting Upscale Customers

Bankers must do more than evaluate the market, however, they must also educate their potential markets about financial planning services. At first this task may seem easier imagined than accomplished. But customers *can* be attracted and educated by banks to use their financial planning services. Since Donald R. Noland, vice president of the Society National Bank of Cleveland's executive and professional department, formed a joint venture with the International Management Group to provide financial planning, 1,200 upscale clients have been attracted to his bank. More than 1,000 account relationships had been set up in the Cleveland area alone, and another 3,000 in various parts of Ohio.

These results are impressive in their own right, but the success in attracting upscale customers doesn't end there. Society National Bank of Cleveland has also established business relationships with more than a dozen of the city's largest corporations. Other businesses continue to request information about Society's financial planning services.

While the interest in financial planning may cross all geographic lines, it is important to determine the demographics of the specific market you plan to attack. As an initial, inexpensive marketing exercise, bankers can gather information about their potential client base — including population trends, household sizes, income and ages — through newspapers, local planning agencies, chambers of commerce, transportation departments and area professional associations. Nor should you overlook your own best source of data. To get a rough idea of your potential financial planning market, you should next consider evaluating customer deposit balances and credit statements. Additional information gathered from bank employees can help clarify the kind of customer you're likely to encounter and the kind of services he or she may need.

Measuring the Potential Market — The 10% of 20% Rule

Once you have this data, how do you translate it into hard business projections? Marilyn MacGruder Barnewall of the market research firm, the MacGruder Agency in Denver, uses "the 10% of 20% Rule" to measure the potential financial planning market among a bank's customers. It works like this:

First, assume that 20 percent of a bank's customers will typically provide 80 percent of the bank's deposits. Half of those are likely to be the "active" bank customers who would probably rather rely on their own abilities to manage their financial assets than to give that responsibility to the bank. The remaining 10 percent are likely to be a prime target for the financial planning services you want to offer.

Market Receptivity

Based on these and other studies, there is little question that the market is ready for banks to offer financial planning services. Increased consumer concern, awareness, and desire for guidance about personal finance management have all made financial planning one of the newest buzzwords in the financial services industry. The single most important impetus pushing banks into the financial planning business comes from consumers who want to do a better job of managing their personal assets.

Consumers are pleading with financial institutions to offer them financial planning services. But they're also concerned about who gives them the service. Who do they consider capable of giving good financial advice?

In 1980, the Stanford Research Institute (SRI) published a study entitled "Household Differentiation of Financial Institutions." It looked at this very question. (See table 2.2.)

It is interesting, but not surprising, that among all households, banks ranked number one out of the vendors who were considered qualified to provide sound financial planning. Perhaps some of this has to do with the solid reputation that banks have had with their customers.

In a recent focus group study conducted by Chemical Bank, the results differed somewhat from the SRI study. Chemical found that accountants are perceived as the best source of overall financial advice. Banks, however, continued to rank very high. (See table 2.3.)

Banks occupy this favorable position in the marketplace for a simple reason: the integrity and objectivity they are perceived to hold. The market's perception of their stability, even in the wake of well-publicized bank failures, also adds to the lending institution's strong market position. Used correctly, this perception could offer a significant competitive advantage over other financial planning providers including insurance companies, brokerage firms, and independent planners. It is much easier for a lending institution to develop expertise than it would have been to develop a reputation for fairness and integrity. However, since competitors are working to increase their reputations in the marketplace, the banks' competitive advantage will not be an endless blessing.

But trustworthiness is not all that banks have going for them as they enter the marketplace. They also have the "bricks and mortar," the physical structures that customers have been going to for bank services for years. Their physical presence in neighborhoods and shopping areas add a measure of convenience that no other competitor can match.

Table 2.1   Chemical Bank's Focus Group Market Segmentation

By Age	Total	< 35	35–54	55+
Overall Interest	24%	27%	27%	10%
Bank Officer = Good Source	41%	43%	37%	48%
Information & Advice Desired On:				
Investments	76%	85%	75%	64%
Taxes	74%	77%	75%	67%
Retirement	66%	65%	77%	48%
Special Needs	55%	69%	55%	33%
Insurance	48%	50%	55%	30%
Estate Planning	64%	60%	67%	67%

By Income	Total	$30M–50	$50M–70	$70M+
Overall Interest	24%	22%	42%	19%
Bank Good Source	41%	49%	42%	15%
Information & Advice Desired on:				
Investments	76%	73%	80%	83%
Taxes	74%	74%	66%	92%
Retirement	66%	63%	77%	67%
Special Needs	55%	55%	70%	25%
Insurance	48%	49%	50%	42%
Estate Planning	64%	66%	57%	83%

Source: "Defining The Market/Packaging The Product." Speech delivered by James B. Shanahan, Chemical Bank, at the Banking Law Institute, March 25–26, 1985.

Table 2.2   Household Differentiation of Financial Institutions
Stanford Research Institute, 1980

Vendors Considered Qualified to Provide a Good Financial Plan	All Households	Rank	Top 2% By Income	Rank
Bank	**57%**	**1**	**44%**	**3**
Independent Planner	54%	2	65%	1
Accountant	40%	3	45%	2
Any Major Financial Firm That Hired Good Staff	31%	4	27%	5
Lawyer	30%	5	38%	4
Insurance Company	29%	6	20%	7
Stock Brokerage Firm	20%	7	22%	6
None	14%	8	16%	8
Finance Company Representative	11%	9	4%	9

Prior Relationships

Most of the respondents to a survey titled, "Keys to a Changing Securities World," which was prepared by the Securities Industry Association and Arthur Andersen & Co., believed that neither financial planning nor venture capital would become dominated by banks or securities firms. Rather, prior relationships with customers would be an important factor determining where customers would go for financial planning services.

In choosing a financial institution, respondents seemed to feel that prior relationships and the institution's soundness and stability would determine their choices. Although current bank customers who are fairly active with their banking transactions may not be the

Table 2.3   Chemical Bank's Focus Group Study

| Type of Advice | *People's Sources of Financial Information and Advice* | | | | |
	Accountants	*Financial Planners*	***Bank Officers***	*Stock Brokers*	*Insurance Agents*
Tax Matters	82%	10%	**6%**	7%	7%
Best Interest Rates	26%	14%	**52%**	12%	3%
Investment Strategies	22%	21%	**14%**	50%	8%
Saving For Retirement	37%	20%	**25%**	12%	15%
Appropriate Insurance	9%	13%	**5%**	2%	73%

Best Overall Source of Financial Advice
Excellent/Good

	Excellent/Good
Accountants	66%
Financial Planners	47%
Bank Officers	**44%**
Stock Brokers	38%
Insurance Agents	35%

Ranking of Key Attributes

	Objective	Expert	Confidential
Accountants	75%	73%	77%
Bank Officers	**55%**	**52%**	**68%**
Financial Planners	53%	51%	59%
Stock Brokers	41%	50%	54%
Insurance Agents	38%	46%	56%

Source: "Defining The Market/Packaging The Product," James B. Shanahan, Chemical Bank. Speech delivered at the Banking Law Institute, March 25–26, 1985.

best market for new bank services, these tend to be in the minority. The customer who simply allows his or her money to sit in one or more accounts, on the other hand, typically has a great deal of trust for your bank. This person might represent a very large untapped market for the new financial planning services — as much as 80 percent of your customer base. Typically, this customer is someone who is willing to become involved and stay committed to the financial institution for the long term; marketing becomes a matter of introducing the service and educating walk-in customers about it.

What the Market Wants

As banks identify the market, it would be a good idea to have a clear picture of what that market wants. Chemical Bank, a forerunner in offering bank financial planning services, found in its survey that potential customers were most interested in the following things:

planning investment strategies — 76%

keeping taxes down — 74%

saving money for retirement — 66%

estate planning — 65%

saving for special needs — 55%

insurance planning — 42%

Competition and Deregulation

Competition is driving banks to capture a market for financial planning services. Rather than relying on customers to find the bank, banks must take an active role in competing for the prospective business.

The change in bankers' attitudes has begun to take hold. Over the last several years, bankers' concerns have shifted to include lack of expertise in financial planning and regulatory constraints that separate banking from the securities and insurance businesses at the top of the list. Add to this the increasing trend towards deregulation, and banks' competitive drives are enhanced even more.

Securities firms, banks, and other financial institutions will fight to gain a foothold in the financial planning arena. In the next several years the competition is almost certain to become more intense. A varied array of financial institutions will struggle to carve out a market share of financial planning customers.

Overall Strategic Plan Mesh

Bankers should carefully plan for an entry into the financial planning marketplace. They should ask themselves:

- How long will it take for customers to adapt to the financial planning product?
- How much of a market will the bank need to make money?
- What kind of promotion should be used?
- Can we identify our program's prime selling points?
- Are there obstacles the bank must overcome to offer financial planning?
- How should we deliver the product?
- Should we purchase or develop the service in house?
- What staffing and training requirements will we face?
- How should we price the service — straight fee, compensating balances, a combination of the two strategies?

It is also generally agreed that financial planning services should not be viewed as short-term solutions to add to a bank's bottom line, but rather as long-term solutions to strengthen the foundation of the bank's customer base and long-range profitability.

Bankers must determine if offering financial planning services is complementary to their bank's long-term strategic plans and profitability. Since smaller banks have restricted budgets, they must determine if the development of a financial planning product is worth the investment.

Services and Fees

The pricing of any financial planning services offered by a financial institution relies heavily on the value the marketplace places on

Table 2.4   Financial Planning Services: Services and Fees

	Client Group	Typical Fee Range
Custom Service 1-2-3-4 Financial data assembled by professionals In-depth analysis made on case-by-case basis Extensive personal consultation available from planners, lawyers, and/or accountants Team approach	CEO, COO, CFO Senior corporate executives typically earning $125,000 or more Owners of closely held business Individuals with high incomes and/or high net worth	$15,000 and up $4,000 to $10,000 per executive for initial planning; about $5,000 annually for updates (fees usually paid by corporation). $10,000 and up depending on the complexity of the case; ongoing annual fees 30 to 40 percent of the initial fee, but may vary considerably.
Executive Seminars 1-2-3 Held at Corporation for groups of 20 to 100 Offer analysis of planning pitfalls typical for such groups Limited personal consultation	Middle Management Executives typically earning $50,000 or more	$600–$800 per executive, usually paid by corporation.

Basic Broker's Service — 4

Data assembled by client with steer from broker   Households with incomes of $40,000 or more $500–$600

Analysis made either by firm's own planners or outside consultants (both of whom rely heavily on computer programs)

Limited consultation with registered rep

The Mass Market — 2-4-5-6

Data assembled by client or planner   Individuals — $40,000 plus $250–$2,500
                                         Households — $75,000–90,000

Personal consultation and implementation

Data assembled by client and analyzed by computer   Households with incomes of $25,000 or more $25–$175

No personal consultation

Major Providers
1 — Interdisciplinary Financial Planning Firms
2 — Banks
3 — Accounting Firms
4 — Brokerage Firms
5 — Computer financial planning firms, who often market through banks and brokerage firms.
6 — Independent Financial Planners

Source: Sam Smyth, National Manager, Royal Trust Corp., Toronto

those services. The services and fees can vary widely, depending on the market an institution is trying to reach. You can get an idea of the range of services and fees by consulting table 2.4, "Financial Planning Services: Services and Fees" on pages 22–23.

Costs will also play a big role in determining the pricing structure of financial planning services. The biggest of these will probably involve the planner. The average income for independent financial planners is between $75,000 and $100,000 a year, and many earn much more. The structural alternatives will be discussed in detail in a later chapter, but if the bank or savings and loan association chooses to work through a joint venture or outside relationship, this cost will be borne by the customer in the form of fees and (perhaps) commissions. If not, support staff may run an additional $20,000 to $30,000 a year in salaries; computer hardware and software, amortized over five years, may run $3,000 to $5,000; overhead, perhaps $5,000 to $7,500; supplies, $2,500; and marketing costs will inevitably run into the thousands.

Since few planners can handle more than 40 individual plans at a time, with only 40 percent of those being new clients, a breakeven price would come to roughly $3,500 per plan for each of the 40 clients; ongoing plans are generally less labor-intensive and more profitable. Where does this fit into the current market? The larger fee-only firms, such as Asset Management Group in Denver; Spoor, Behrins, Campbell & Young in New York; and Ayco/American Express in Albany, NY all typically charge between $5,000 and $7,500 for the basic planning services, which may involve a team of lawyers and some custom designed investment products. Independent planners, many of whom receive the bulk of their compensation via commissions, will charge between $500 and $2,000, depending on the plan's complexity. At the low end of the pricing scale, some of the larger Wall Street firms offer computerized plans with boilerplate text for $200 to $500.

Two other aspects of pricing should be considered in passing. First, the financial plan can be expected to generate additional revenues upon implementation, which will show up in the discount brokerage operations, and in sales to and custodial fees within a retirement account. Also, not all bank customers require the comprehensive service that an independent planner offers his best customers. Security Pacific, in Los Angeles, has been very successful offering a "bullet" approach to the service: the client receives answers to specific questions, and is charged by the hour.

Thus, if the bank doesn't feel that the market will bear a $3,500 fee, it has several options to reduce the price. One, obviously, is to factor in the plan's value as a sales tool, and use the planning process to aggressively sell bank-related services. Another is to joint venture with a local planner, offering him or her a chance to increase his or her customer base, but leaving his or her overhead outside of your corporate balance sheet. As we will see in a later chapter, this arrangement can be structured to the bank's advantage, even to the point of enlisting the planner as a part-time bank representative. Or the lending institution could enter into a relationship with a "turn key" service provider which would, among other things, offer customized investment products and access to low-cost computerized planning capabilities. Under a joint venture, the plan's cost could be brought down to the $1,000 range — lower if subsidized by sales of commissionable non-bank-related investment products to the customer. Under a "turnkey" situation, the bank's plan would be less comprehensive but much cheaper — one vendor offers 12 or 14 components for $50-$100 each, and allows for a profit margin for the bank on each plan sold.

3

Setting Up Shop — Inside or Out?

They were afraid of exposing their deposit base, but it's silly to live with your head in the sand. Sophisticated investors at any bank are going to make their money work for them, so the obvious thing is to provide a service that will help them reach their goals. At the same time, you create loans and fee income from other bank services.

Robert C. Quigley, President
First Interstate Bank
New Mexico

Mandates for Success

Over the past several years, many financial institutions have moved into financial planning. No two efforts have been alike. They share, however, certain common mandates that define success in the marketplace.

1. Commitment to objective, top-quality financial planning must come from the top. Bank CEOs have agreed to adequate funding often after they've examined well-thought-out business plans. Many times these CEOs have gone through the planning process themselves, so they have a thorough understanding of it.

2. Every department in the bank has been both briefed on the financial planning service and taught how to prospect for customers.

3. The planning operation itself is staffed by well-trained people with enough expertise to provide a quality service. Their compensation, which often includes incentives, is high enough to retain them.

4. The planning department receives strong administrative support and works closely with the marketing department to devise methods of bringing in customers.

5. The legal department has structured contracts for the planning service.

6. The bank has obtained adequate insurance, usually an errors and omissions policy, to protect it from potential customer suits.

The dissimilarities are perhaps even more striking. Banks in larger communities have aimed their planning services at specific customer groups, some targeting high net worth individuals and others going after a true middle-class market. Smaller banks, with smaller numbers of potential customers, have created shotgun marketing approaches, trying to hit as much of the market as possible. Where the service is located within the bank and how it fits into the organization is not fixed. In short, if you can imagine an arrangement, it is probably being tried.

Financial planning at community banks is taking place in new accounts departments, retail departments, and trust and commercial divisions. Some truly innovative stand-alone units combine a group of formerly separate bank functions under a planning banner, or they have direct, red-tape cutting links to other departments. Client conferences take place everywhere from boardrooms to living rooms — anywhere that bank planners feel they achieve some level of privacy and propriety.

Because some operations rely heavily on computers, they have spent thousands of dollars for state-of-the-art financial planning software. Others, however, have determined that all they need is Lotus 1-2-3 or another spreadsheet program.

Salaries for planners and support personnel vary all over the lot — from a low of barely $20,000 to $60,000 or more. Planning-oriented banks have frequently experimented with incentive compensation. Annual costs also vary widely, depending largely on whether a bank has gone into planning on its own or formed a joint venture with an outside provider.

Preliminary Decisions

Considering all these differences, it is clear that banks should not enter into financial planning lightly. Deciding which way to go on basic issues will require many preliminary decisions and much assessing of alternative configurations.

- Who will the planners report to?
- How much overhead should go into the planning department budget?
- Which of the growing number of outside planning support services fit best with what a bank wants to do?
- Will those service companies be around in three to five years to ensure continuity?
- Should tracking systems be set up (and if so, how) to follow business generated by the planning unit?
- Which department should receive income credit for that business?
- Is it wise to use planning personnel for other bank tasks?

- How should other bank departments be introduced to and educated about the service?
- Who inside the bank is best qualified to move into a planning role?
- Where can qualified planners be found?

Some money center banks now offering planning spent as much as four man years analyzing these and a host of other options before designing their planning programs. Some of the early community banks who entered the financial planning business early spent months experimenting before settling on comfortable formulas.

Fortunately for bankers still at the thinking stage of setting up financial planning services, much of what these pioneers have learned is readily available through magazine articles, a growing number of conferences, and through financial planning industry groups. Experienced assistance may be obtained through a limited but growing number of consultants.

Banks and other financial institutions must make some fundamental decisions about setting up financial planning services. Among these are whether to offer the service on their own or to join with an outside firm. There is not one single answer that promises success for all banks. Each alternative has its pros and cons, problems and advantages.

Internal Programs

Bankers Systems (Box 97, St. Cloud, MN 56302, 800-328-2342), one of the largest community bank service companies in the country, has designed a financial planning/workshop program with the needs of the smaller lending institution in mind. The service as originally conceived involved training and licensing of bank personnel, modular computerized plans with a profit for the bank, custom-designed investment products and marketing support. At one time the program was unique in the market. Today, however, bankers who take the trouble to investigate, will find a growing number of planning support services that can fill specific niches.

These support services generally fall into the following categories: back office plan production, record keeping and planning software for internal use, franchised planning packages, seminars, workshops, and other marketing tools.

Except for planning software, now offered by at least fifty different companies, the support market for banks trying to set up their own financial planning shops is not crowded. Major bank service companies like Federated Investors, and more recently Fidelty, are only looking at planning support services. SEI Corporation, a $90 million bank software company based in Wayne, Pennsylvania, has begun preliminary work on planning software. If the final product at all resembles the company's trust support packages, it will be extensive. The Bankers Systems seminars are based largely on part of a total planning system available through The Mandell Institute in Storrs, Connecticut. Mandell also offers training for bank officers. EQUITEC, a San Francisco-based financial services firm has hired former comptroller C. Todd Conover to create a new planning service for bankers and savings and loan officers to offer their clients.

When it comes to back office operations — companies that process plans at centralized computer facilities — bankers will find considerably more choice. The two leading companies in this area are Consumer Financial Institute of Newton, Massachusetts, which has worked with more than 200 banks, professional organizations, major corporations, and other financial services companies, and the COAP division of Cali Computer Systems. The latter company, based in Greenvale, Long Island, has sold its Moneymaster software to a number of banks which in turn are churning out 90-page plans that sell for under $100. It also has on-line capability to accept client data and generate three different levels of plans, each of increasing complexity. In early 1985, COAP introduced a program to make this type of service available to home banking customers.

More recent entrants into this market include Bank of Boston (through its 51 percent-owned Quissett Corporation subsidiary) and Computer Language Research Corporation of Dallas. The Quissett Plan, now in use at several major banks and a number of smaller institutions, is a well-written, mildly entertaining document that usually retails for $495. The company suggests bankers can use it as a final product, as a building block for more complex final products, or as a data gathering and number crunching tool never seen by the customer. Bank of Boston was selling a package of training for bank employees, marketing support and development, and the datalink hookup for around $25,000. The Computer Language service comes through the company's FASTTAX division, which owns a leading market share in computerized tax return preparation. Even though the plan preparation service is aimed primarily at CPAs, we believe banks could use it successfully ($195 enrollment and $95 per plan).

Quissett also offers a financial planning program aimed directly at banks, but bankers may be better off not using this service because the computerized plan it contains is less comprehensive than many others, as well as biased in favor of bank products. In an increasingly competitive environment, bankers seeking to enter financial planning must be prepared to "do it right" or they will wind up losing business to competitors who are more customer-needs-oriented.

There are many choices of personal computer financial planning software available, ranging in price from under $100 to $5,000 or more. Larger community banks, which expect to do 100 or more plans a year, should take a look at so-called "expert system" financial planning software, first introduced to the market late in 1985 by the Cambridge, Massachusetts-based Applied Experts Systems. This program amounts to a sophisticated planner in a box. Although it sounds impossible, preliminary tests indicate that the program works and works well. You'll have to determine for yourself whether or not it is worth its hefty price tag.

When considering how to structure an internally mounted planning program, bankers should recognize that none of these outside services need be used. Armed with good spreadsheet and word processing programs, which most banks already have, perfectly adequate plans can be turned out by a well-qualified planner. Buying a good planning software program, however, may be less expensive than hiring a planner. Most software can also be used as an on-the-job training tool for bank personnel.

Setting up internal financial planning units within banks need not be an expensive undertaking. If a bank is starting from scratch, it should figure on first year funding of between $75,000 and $250,000. These budget parameters include all associated costs: personnel, computer hardware and software, administrative support, marketing, and general overhead.

Even if bank CEOs can justify that kind of outlay for an uncertain return, however, they will face a number of significant problems in setting up internal operations. The largest hurdle will be finding personnel capable of providing high-quality planning. Most banks do not have adequately trained planners on staff. Trust officers and experienced customer service officers come closest, but even though these people often possess well-developed counseling skills, they almost invariably lack much of the knowledge about investment products and tax and legal strategies required to do comprehensive planning.

Bankers determined to use their own people can provide training through the College for Financial Planning, the American College in Bryn Mawr, Pennsylvania, or a growing number of programs at colleges and universities. Appendix V, lists affiliated colleges and universities offering courses leading to the CFP designation. Many of the planning service companies also provide training programs as part of their marketing efforts. There are also consultants.

Because the necessary expertise is so broadbased (tax law, investments, life and other types of insurance, gifting and other legal strategies), it often takes several years to acquire. Even a particularly competent individual working at breakneck speed should figure on months of learning. Allowing an individual who has started training to begin doing planning work for customers could easily lead to errors, poor advice, disgruntled (and therefore lost) customers, and even potential liability.

The staffing alternative — hiring a planner from outside — also has its difficulties. Not only are qualified financial planners still relatively rare throughout the country (probably no more than 30,000) most of them are highly entrepreneurial. Banks should expect to pay dearly to get one or more of them to move into a corporate environment. Starting salaries for experienced personnel range upwards from $60,000. Even planners with full qualifications but limited experience can command $35,000 to $40,000.

A further hurdle involves the regulatory aspects of offering financial planning services, a topic discussed at length in chapters 5 and 6. Although considerably less vexing than it was two or three years ago (now that a number of banks have blazed trails in what was uncharted territory), dealing with regulatory authorities and getting them to pass on proposed activities will still eat up time and resources.

Finally, because the entire process of setting up financial planning takes months, sometimes years to accomplish, given the ongoing demands of running a bank, bankers may be better off going the joint venture route to get in fast while the getting is good. As competition increases and more customer relationships are locked up, the cost/benefit ratio of this new business will begin to decline.

Joint Ventures

Joint ventures with outside planning firms can work quite well. (See case studies in Appendix VI.) They are by no means limited to situations where a bank has a large enough group of high net worth individuals in its marketing area to justify concentrating on a high-end service.

Bankers do have problems to overcome in setting up joint ventures, however. The regulatory picture for joint ventures, for example, may be even more complex than it is for internal programs. Bankers looking at joint ventures also must enter negotiations prepared to work out a two-way deal, as well as trust an outsider (over whom they have no control) to discharge his or her responsibilities in a professional manner that will protect the bank from the risk that is inherent in financial planning.

Both parties in the joint ventures we have studied have had something to gain. The bank gets low cost, speedy entry into a profitable new business which it can very suddenly provide with considerable expertise. The financial planner gets access to a large potential block of customers, which will drastically cut the planner's marketing expenses. Because both parties have a greater interest in the success of the venture than its failure, they cooperate and both profit. If the very notion of letting some "commission salesperson" loose in your fileroom gives you the shakes, however, you should probably not consider entering into a joint venture with any but fee-only planners or local accounting firms.

Finding a quality outside planner is no easy task. In spite of the huge numbers of people claiming to offer financial planning today, not all have the broad-based expertise and experience that a banker should demand.

Good places to start looking are local IAFP chapters, local CPA firms, large insurance agencies, and brokerage houses.

What to Expect of a Joint Venture

Barker French is president of The Hub Financial Services, a Pittsburgh-based fee-only financial planning firm which has negotiated relationships with several major banks. French is also a former banker, having served as a trust officer at Mellon Bank in the 1970s. He offers some suggestions about what a bank should expect of a joint venture relationship. "First of all," he says, "confidentiality must be promised. Bankers should expect the planner to make their customer relationships better, not to disturb them. For example, if a planner uncovers customer dissatisfaction with some aspect of his partner bank's operations, he should encourage the client to go back and work them out. Second, planners should be willing to lend their credibility to the bank's marketing effort. They can do this by allowing their names to be used in the title of the planning company and in association with marketing materials. Also, bankers can realistically expect planners to refer customer clients back to the bank for products and services provided they are competitive in price and quality."

Nelson Neiman of Roe, Martin & Neiman, an Atlanta-based planning firm that has also worked with banks, believes bankers should look for good professional credentials and a solid long-term track record of investment expertise. "Banks getting into planning, particularly for upscale customers, are often concerned that their reputations as investment advisors are weak in some areas," he says. "Customers of a Texas bank, for instance, expect expertise in oil and gas, but maybe not in real estate. In the Midwest bankers know agriculture well, but as recent performance suggests, they know little about energy. Once they begin to offer planning, they quickly discover the marketing advantages inherent in the reputation of the outside firm."

Most community bankers will be aiming financial planning at a broader, more middle-class market whose members will refuse, according to most financial consumer research, to pay much more than 1 percent of their annual gross income for financial advice. What that means in joint venture terms is alliance with a planning firm which earns commissions only or which earns both fees and commissions. Having the courage to charge fees for advice is one characteristic of a professional. There are, however, extremely ethical, highly competent planners who continue to work on a commission-only basis.

Another characteristic is a strong set of credentials. By this we don't mean a college diploma or brass plaques awarded by mutual fund companies and other financial product manufacturers to hot shot salespeople. Bankers should look for planners who have persevered with continuing education and have earned the CFP or ChFC designation. CPAs, MBAs, JDs, and other professional degrees are also good credentials if the individual has several years of planning experience.

Structuring a Joint Venture

One advantage for a bank of working with a planner who earns commissions is the ability to share in those revenues, provided the joint venture is properly structured. Bankers and planners can work out a mutually profitable and comfortable relationship, but for newcomers the process of structuring a relationship might seem the most difficult part of working with outside planners.

We're not talking about legal structure. Enough holes have now been poked in banking regulation to allow bankers and planners who want to work together to do so easily, provided they have adequate legal counsel. From both sides of the equation, the difficult issue revolves around trust.

Bankers can check the professional qualifications of planners forever and enroll attorneys to draft protective agreements, but as most successful planners know, nine times out of ten, a bank customer who becomes a planning client will develop first loyalty to the planner. Bankers must simply learn to trust that a relationship with an honorable, competent outside planner will bring in business, and that the planner will try to maintain his or her relationship with the bank because it is a rich source of clients.

Among the alternative joint ventures being used are a separate joint venture (See Case Study 4, Appendix VI, focusing on the Missouri Savings-P & W venture.); space leases with rent calculated as a percentage of revenues, fee-sharing (See Case Study 1, Appendix VI, focusing on First Interstate & Pennington Bass.); and no participation at all by the bank in planning fees or commissions. In the last case, bankers derive revenue from having planning clients referred back to the bank for available services. By carefully identifying the planning service with the bank, banks strengthen their ties with customers.

"Planner-banker cooperation works best," says Lee Pennington, an independent planner who has worked with banks since the mid-1970s, "if the bank's commitment comes from the top." Clearly that is true when problems crop up in a relationship. No formal agreement to work together covers all of the details of cooperative marketing, for example, or inconvenient contingencies.

Using outside financial planners is convenient in the start-up phase of a bank's financial planning services, but eventually bank personnel can learn enough planning to handle the needs of middle income customers, provided their banks supply strong support tools — mostly computers and financial planning software. For example, Preston State Bank in Dallas, which in 1984 started providing planning to private banking customers in conjunction with the local office of Arthur Young, the Big Eight accounting firm, developed plans within months after the program began to add an in-house financial planner for less complicated cases. The most logical individual to move into that role is a person who has acted as a financial planning coordinator, screening potential planning clients and making referrals to the bank's outside planners. As this person develops expertise, the bank may decide to cut off all contact with its original partner. Bankers negotiating with outside planners should recognize and deal with this possibility by drafting a buy-out clause or some other arrangement.

Using the Joint Venture to Move In-House

An arrangement that starts with bank employees presenting plans to customers, even though they were prepared by an outside firm, will sooner or later evolve into the bankers doing more of the planning themselves, if only because they'll need the actual preparation experience to maximize the effectiveness of their presentations. A bank may use a joint venture with an outside firm as a low cost method to test its market, and then begin to move the planning activity into the bank once the demand is proven.

Chances are, however, that most banks will always need some access to outsiders, if only for their investment expertise. Consulting agreements with former outside planners may become common in a few years as more banker-planner relationships mature.

Bank employees, largely trained by the planner either directly or through example, will take over the actual planning, but they will continue to rely on his or her knowledge of investments, particularly in the tax shelter area. Banks could forge new ties with manufacturers of this type of product, and, provided demand from their planning clientele was large enough, actually order wholesale to preagreed specifications rather than buying off the shelf. Major money center banks, like Wells Fargo and Security Pacific, have already moved in this direction. It would be logical that community planning banks will follow suit, although naturally on a smaller scale. To plan for this, a good place to start looking for new partners is among commercial customers in the real estate, energy, agriculture, communications, and transportation business — the five traditional sources for direct investment products.

"Some banks will probably never have an inside planning department or at most they'll have skeleton staff to interface with planning clients," says Steve Scherer of The Private Financial Counseling Group in Los Angeles. Scherer, a former money center bank planner, has worked with a number of banks in various joint venture and consulting capacities. All banks new to planning, he believes, need help getting into the business, understanding how to position a planning service within their total operations, and identifying niches to service in their local markets — the kind of information that is only available from experienced planners.

Scherer thinks that many banks will never be able to justify the cost of an in-house planning department, especially for comprehensive work, because profits in planning are low compared to profits in traditional bank operations. Joint ventures obviously allow the benefits of bolstered customer relationships without using personnel from other departments and sacrificing the higher margin business they would otherwise bring in.

Conclusion

Bankers considering a move into financial planning should start by deciding whether to stay inside or go outside. All other aspects of setting up a financial planning program flow from this decision.

Either route can lead to success. It is getting later in the competitive day, however, and increasingly bankers entering the arena will have more success if they bring along a knowledgeable partner. Not only is going outside clearly less expensive, it is faster. A well-negotiated joint venture will provide almost as many cross-selling opportunities, fees, and new deposits as an entirely internal operation.

Going outside also has the advantage of flexibility. Bankers can pick and choose among the best planners in their geographic area. Nothing prevents the termination of such a relationship after several years.

While it is true that going outside involves some risk, keeping total control and providing less than excellent service is also a risky proposition. A joint venture with a quality planning firm is hardly a one-way street. The planning firm contributes expertise, marketing knowledge, the facility to train bank employees in planning, and its own (not inconsiderable) credibility. Consumers do view banks as trustworthy, according to every survey, but bankers generally have a much higher opinion of their own investment expertise than the general public does.

The trustworthy image is based on the public's confidence in permanence and the soundness of the banking system. It is not based on a historical record of helping people achieve financial goals. As independent financial planners rapidly achieve the status of professionals over the next half decade, they will preempt this position, if they have not done so already. Bankers who choose to go it alone will find their marketing task arduous.

This is not to say that staying inside won't work. By carefully selecting planning support services, bankers can get some of the benefits (training, rapid entry, and possibly credibility) of a joint venture. In local markets without competent outsiders (There are many smaller banks with opportunity in these.), it is the better choice.

Bankers' major competitive advantage in the financial services war now raging is their credibility. In moving into planning, this intangible asset should be zealously protected. From broad experience with people who call themselves "financial planners," we can testify that the jungle is currently full of charlatans, albeit well meaning ones in some cases.

While it undoubtedly would be safest for bankers thinking about planning to wait until the market and their profession settle down into some established order, this course is not the most prudent. Competition increases daily. Whichever route is taken after careful consideration, bankers are clearly better off riding with the growing momentum of financial planning than standing puzzled at the fork in the road.

Competition in Financial Planning

But difficulties haven't been confined to banks. Major players in the insurance and securities sectors have also had their share of performance problems. The more intense competitive pressures have taken a toll on margins in these businesses, just as in banking. As a result, there is now less room for error in management decisions to expand product lines or enter new markets.

Anthony M. Solomon, President
Federal Reserve Bank of New York
Remarks to National Bankers Association,
10/17/84

Expansion of Financial Planning Services

Since the 1960s when a few financial services professionals (some insurance salespeople, some brokers, some CPAs, and even some bankers) became dissatisfied with their limited traditional roles and began providing a total service called "financial planning" to their clients, the movement toward customer or market driven strategies and away from product or capital driven strategies in financial services has expanded to every type of financial services company that deals with consumers. Largely because of advances in information technology, which have created operating efficiencies for providers of financial services and a markedly better informed and more sophisticated consumer, the money business has undergone a metamorphosis. Where well-established boundaries once kept depository institutions, insurance companies, accounting firms, and securities brokers on their own turf, today all types of financial services companies compete for consumers' total business. Firms of every size and description have created products and begun delivering services formerly the province of other types of firms. These companies are increasingly discovering the power of the financial planning process as a total delivery mechanism in their recently transformed companies.

Financial planning has become a buzzword in today's financial services environment. Industry giants like Prudential-Bache and IDS/ American Express have spent tens of millions of advertising dollars popularizing the expression. Thousands of insurance agents, stock brokers, tax shelter salespeople, CPAs and bankers claim to provide the service. Whether the burgeoning market for financial planning represents latent consumer demand or the result of the combined marketing efforts of all these players is largely academic. What is important about this service is that it works, provided that it is not abused. By abuse we mean promising more than is delivered or than ever was intended to be delivered; in short, using financial planning for the immediate, short-term benefit of its provider rather than the long-term benefit of customers. There are banks and thrifts in various parts of the country selling "financial plans" designed primarily to bring in deposits, but apparently, neither the plans nor the bank personnel who deliver them to customers pay any attention to a much more important issue: namely, whether the customer's overall financial health will be improved by doing more business with the bank.

Financial planning is, and probably always will be, an inexact science with various practitioners disagreeing on the fine points of how best to redistribute assets for maximum achievement of a given client's goals, but it is quite clear that instead of plopping all their funds into a passbook account, a NOW account, or CDs, nearly all Americans would be better off investing in a diversified group of products appropriate to their risk tolerance and selected to help them reach defined and clearly understood financial goals. For two very basic and undeniable reasons — a customer demand for competent advice and increasing competition in the marketplace — bankers and any of their financial services competitors who attempt to subvert the purpose of financial planning to their own immediate ends, will ultimately fail.

Competent Advice and Increasing Competition

Study after study, beginning with the landmark work of Stanford Research Institute (now SRI International) has found that Americans want straight, competent, trustworthy advice about their financial affairs. This demand is increasing in power and extent as financial sophistication diffuses through more and more layers of the population.

Competition also continues to grow. Most bankers in touch with their communities are well aware that mounting numbers of local insurance agents, stockbrokers, and CPAs are offering financial planning services to customers of their banks. Chances are that some of these former salespeople now claim to be financial planners and support their assertion with a bewildering variety of new credentials available.

By mid-1985, the IAFP had more than 22,000 members in over 100 local chapters. About two-thirds of these considered themselves financial planners. *The Wall Street Journal* and other publications frequently estimate the number of people calling themselves planners between 150,000 and 200,000. Prime-time television advertising slots have increasingly been filled with messages about financial planning from Sears, Prudential-Bache, CIGNA, and others. Financial services companies of all types and sizes, from the smallest community bank to the nation's largest insurance companies, have almost uniformly and within the space of a scant few years realigned their products and started making financial planning services available to Americans of almost every economic group.

The entrance of major financial services companies into the planning market has also had a decided impact on the overall quality orientation of the profession. The CEO of Metropolitan Life or Chemical Bank can hardly consider jeopardizing his or her firm's reputation, built up over decades, by instructing his or her personnel to give inexact, incomplete advice to customers simply to squeeze out a few more dollars of profit. Thanks to ever more probing media and the rapid dissemination of information no chicanery can last for long. It was one thing to lose a customer twenty or thirty years ago in a slower moving world. Usually you had the opportunity to win him or her back at a later date. But today, when the number of competitors has increased dramatically and almost all of them have the resources to tie up that lost customer in a total, enduring financial relationship, only foolish executives are willing to take the risk of thinking of their companies before thinking of their customers.

Insurance Companies

Why should a bank try to compete with such formidable giants as life insurance companies? Bankers should not lapse into despair at the prospect. There are chinks in the armor of these huge companies. For one thing, insurance companies today are fighting an uphill battle against the widespread perception that they will do just about anything to sell more insurance. With the marketplace increasingly demanding quality, this image is a distinct disadvantage.

While the most successful planning efforts at life insurance companies have strictly segregated the advisory and sales functions, first helping clients plan how to achieve their goals and only later attempting to supply them with products where appropriate (CIGNA is probably the best example), these undertakings require extremely expensive training and support programs and take years to put in place. While insurors' public relations people work on polishing their industry's image, and trainers spend years teaching agents how to use mutual funds, real estate partnerships, and the host of other investment products companies have added to their shelves, there exists a window of opportunity. A recent study of insurance industry trends by Arthur Andersen and the Life Office Management Association includes the prediction by top insurance executives that by the end of the decade financial planners will create more insurance business than any other group, including specialist career agents. More important for bankers, the same study concludes that banks will play a larger and larger role in the distribution of insurance products over the next decade.

All life insurance companies — those which have determined to be pure manufacturing operations as well as those committed to their career agents — have begun exploring alternative distribution methods. In a more competitive environment this is a practical necessity. For bankers who want to compete aggressively it is an opportunity. Whether it requires a joint venture, some other arrangement, or even the development of a new type of insurance product, bankers should investigate the possibility of working with insurance companies.

CPAs

For a profession entranced by exactitude and rigid adherence to rules, public accounting's growing fascination with financial planning is a strange affair indeed. Many CPAs have recognized that planning could be a true sweetheart business, what with its growing popularity and ability to lock up clients, but more than any other group to enter the newest financial services profession, public accountants lack the client counseling skills and entrepreneurial flair so necessary for success.

Even though most CPAs have strong technical skills, especially in tax matters, and possess a durable reputation for objectivity (clearly a marketing advantage), few accountants understand even the basic economics of investments unless they've made a special self-educational effort. Those few CPAs who already offer financial planning, however, are rapidly closing this skills gap, as the bulk of those moving into planning will also undoubtedly do in short order.

Although many CPAs who claim to practice planning continue to resist the recognition, their more open-minded compatriots at every level of the profession are beginning to admit that financial planning is more than simply tax planning and a little estate planning. "It's a different ballgame," insists Jim Wilson, a former partner at McGladrey, Hendrickson & Pullen and a member of the recently formed AICPA Personal Financial Planning Committee.

Even if public accountants en masse suddenly relinquished their steadfastly argued position that they have always done financial planning, the profession would still face what could be a greater competitive disadvantage than any skills gap. Public accountants are rigorously self-regulated professionals, and years of obedient adherence to established standards has created a certain inertia which makes it extremely unlikely that CPAs will charge into the financial planning business as long as the many issues relating to ethics, practice standards, objectivity, regulation and independence remain unresolved. To date, little or no guidance has been forthcoming from the Securities and Exchange Commission (SEC), state accountancy boards, or other oversight bodies, and the efforts of industry groups to define and create rules for financial planning by CPAs has only just begun. Given the leisurely historical pace of standard-setting bodies like the American Institute of Certified Public Accountants (AICPA), which established a financial planning committee only in 1985, and the undeniably difficult political issues which accompany the profession's debate about various aspects of financial planning, we expect that years will pass before CPAs receive any definitive guidelines from their industry's leadership.

Nevertheless, interest in financial planning is obviously high among CPAs. Approximately 20 percent of recent inquiries to the AICPA Ethics Committee concern issues involved in providing the service. The 1984–1985 AICPA Financial Planning conferences were among that organization's most successful programs in recent memory. More than 2000, or roughly 10 percent of IAFP members are now CPAs, and CPA enrollments at the College for Financial Planning in Denver increased from 6 percent of fewer than 10,000 in 1982 to 11 percent of over 22,000 enrollees currently pursuing their CFPs. Companies like FASTTAX and Practitioners Publishing Company, which dominate the CPA service market, have moved rapidly to bring out new planning reference products and create planning service bureaus.

These developments make perfect sense when one considers the radical changes that have shaken the economics of public accounting in recent years. For a decade or more, national firms have watched margins in their audit practices decline steadily, and more recently tax practitioners have suddenly found themselves in a commodity business. Due to the widespread application of computer technology, much of the value CPAs once added by drawing on experience and arduously cultivated expertise has become the province of almost anyone with a license to practice, and outsiders as well. The profession initially responded to these changes by developing consulting work (known as management advisory services or MAS), and has since added actuarial and appraisal services, service bureaus for record keeping, and customized computer software, to name but a few of a host of new services. Financial planning is the latest component of this matrix, with most CPAs regarding it as a higher margin business with the potential to strengthen existing relationships, establish new ties with clients of financial services competitors, and cross sell any other services the accounting firm may offer. There is even a strong possibility that financial planning will become the fourth major area of public accounting, achieving equal status with audit, tax, and MAS.

The impact that thousands of CPAs suddenly offering planning services could have on the rest of the financial services industry is enormous. More than 65,000 AICPA members practice on their own or in small firms, and the bulk of their work relates to taxes for individuals and small businesses — all prime candidates for financial planning.

While most observers agree that planning, with its relatively low entry barriers compared to other new areas of CPA practice, is a natural evolution for the profession, any immediate widespread movement into the field remains extremely unlikely. "It will take time for small practitioners to acquire the necessary knowledge in investments and to integrate planning into their firms," notes Ron Meier, a non-practicing CPA and fee-only planner who has taught financial planning courses for the Texas state CPA society, and writes for the *CPA Financial Planner*, a newsletter. (See Case Studies 6 and

7 in Appendix VI for a look at competition from the Big Eight accounting firms and smaller national and large regional firms.)

Brokers

New York Stock Exchange (NYSE) Firms

With the exception of E.F. Hutton, which has one of the largest true financial planning departments in the nation, most Wall Street houses and regional firms have gone through a love-hate relationship with financial planning over the course of the past decade. In the mid-1970s, when brokers were adding scores of new products to their shelves in reaction to the end of set commissions, financial planning looked like a natural distribution vehicle. But almost every firm that set up a department to do quality planning discovered sooner or later that making money with the service was extremely difficult, even after factoring in commissions generated when plans drawn for customers were implemented. In a number of instances, pressure from corporate executives for planning units to use their influence to sell certain products resulted in resignations of conscientious planners, and the units gradually disappeared, particularly when firms were pressed economically during bear markets.

Finally, in June 1982, when Merrill Lynch closed up its Personal Capital Planning Group, it was the end of an era. A few regional firms persisted with planning groups, Hutton's exceptional department continued, and here and there a few well qualified financial planners still worked as brokers, but the companies themselves offered little or no support for these individuals, preferring to ignore their methodology as long as they achieved sales goals.

In place of financial planning, which had proved unworkable, brokerage companies adopted needs oriented selling as the marketing method of the future. In more than one instance these programs have been identified and promoted as financial planning, but they clearly fall short of that. Computer generated "financial plans," like Merrill Lynch's Pathfinder and several at Dean Witter, can do no more than provide buyers general information about inflation, interest rates, and taxes. Current technology simply does not permit the hands-on, in-depth analysis that marks true financial planning. Some of these sales tools are better than others, in that recipients are only mildly rather than vigorously pushed in the direction of buying the sponsoring firm's products, but we know of no case in which one of these products has achieved the sales target established by the company which sells it.

To be fair, these computer-generated plans were conceived with multiple purposes, and there is some evidence that they have succeeded in helping brokerage companies convert some of their salespeople from a strictly transaction mentality to a more client oriented way of thinking. For training new brokers these plans undoubtedly have value, especially if the rest of a firm's training program is based on a needs oriented approach, but we believe that most brokerage houses will need years to convert older, established salespeople to this way of thinking. It's one thing for Merrill's new chairman to talk of making brokers think of the client first, and entirely another to convince an experienced broker making over $100,000 a year that he should ask about client's long range concerns rather than continue to sell the best looking deal of the day.

Bankers should not be frightened of the likes of Prudential-Bache and Sears which are using huge advertising campaigns to convince America that they offer financial planning. These companies are years away from offering anything of the kind on a firmwide basis. The $100,000-plus household income market is well aware that mutual funds, tax shelters, and insurance can be sold in many different ways, and the vast middle market is fast catching up in financial sophistication. On the other hand, it would be foolhardy to dismiss Wall Street's retailing expertise. These companies know investments, some of them know how to train; they possess the best implementation capability in the market; and they operate free of the type of regulatory shackles that continue to hamper bankers. We believe, however, they may continue to suffer competitively from a poor public image and a lack of personal contact between their distribution force and the public. The telephone may allow access but it doesn't necessarily foster confidence, and *confidence in the supplier is the key to success in financial planning.*

Curiously enough, during the past few years, as brokerage house executives moved steadily away from supporting true financial planning, a small but growing number of their brokers began adopting this discipline wholeheartedly for a variety of reasons. Some saw it as the only way to be comfortable with recommending investments to clients, others as a way to coordinate the plethora of investment offerings made available by their firms, and still others simply gravitated to financial planning as the wave of the future. Beginning in 1984 and with stepped up frequency in 1985, these planner/brokers began demanding support from headquarters for the way they were doing business. Most wanted to charge fees for their plans, and have access to state-of-the-art computer planning software and new and better educational opportunities in order to remain competitive with planner/salespeople at other financial services companies. In brief, they told management, "we are doing planning whether you like it or not; support us or we'll leave." It is unclear how this trend will develop. Some companies, like Smith Barney and Paine Webber, have agreed to demands, but others are dragging their feet because of uncertainty over how to maintain control over brokers' advisory activities which could lead to substantial liability.

Regardless of this grass roots movement, the NYSE brokerage firms in general may be the least potent group of competitors in the financial planning industry. Commission income as a percentage of total revenue has been declining for years, and management is likely to become less and less patient with an expensive, inefficient retail distribution system with cyclical profitability. Spending limited capital to upgrade this portion of their businesses appears less and less attractive as competition grows, especially if higher returns can be achieved by devoting resources to investment banking and institutional sales activities.

National Association of Securities Dealers (NASD) Firms

Into this category fall companies like Integrated Resources, Financial Service Corporation, and Financial Planners Equity Corporation, which have grown and prospered over the past decade by acting as broker dealers almost exclusively for financial planners. Like their NYSE counterparts, most NASD firms manufacture investment products and quite a few are also in the life insurance business. But many of the products they carry, and in some cases all of them, are manufactured by others. The primary role of these firms is as an intermediary between manufacturers of financial products and planner/registered representatives who have chosen to use the firm as a conduit for the investment side of their businesses. Perhaps more than any other group, these companies understand the needs of independent planners. Because planners are the fastest growing type of financial services professional, that knowledge represents a strong competitive advantage.

Unlike most other financial services distributors, however, most NASD firms support their sales forces with value-added services rather than paying overhead. Most of these financial planner support organizations spend heavily, for example, on educating their reps about the proper uses of various products in a financial planning context. A growing number have instituted continuing due diligence programs, which allow planners to keep up with the status of investments previously purchased by their clients. Certainly, those firms which most actively support the development of financial planning expertise among their representatives have been the fastest growing and most successful over the past five years.

In competing with banks, insurance companies, and more traditional brokers for share of the distribution market, one of these firms' most significant strengths is in-depth investment knowledge and the ability to know not only which direct investment products will sell but also which will most likely stand the test of time. Thanks to new technology, NASD broker dealers can provide implementation of product solutions as expertly as the largest New York wirehouses, at least on the non-institutional level.

Independent Planners

What truly makes NASD firms a force to be reckoned with over the next decade, however, is the independent planner that they service. He or she is the veteran in the planning business, and indeed, until the past few years was the only widespread source of planning expertise other than small departments at a few major banks and brokerage houses, whose activities were largely limited to a small group of wealthy clients. As the popularity of financial planning has grown, so have the independent's qualifications and expertise. Today the competent, conscientious financial planner is fast approaching professional status. Arguably, he or she is the most potent competitor of all. Bankers should not dismiss him or her in planning their strategies.

Who is this person? Chances are he or she comes from a brokerage or insurance background and continues to earn the majority of his or her compensation from commissions, although IAFP member surveys show a strong and definite trend away from commissions toward fees for advisory service. The same surveys indicate that much of this movement arises from planners' growing desire to be recognized for the professionals they are. The independent's market is primarily the affluent middle class (households with incomes from $50,000 to $125,000). The planner spends almost a tenth of his or her working time every year improving analytical skills and product knowledge in order to better serve clients.

He or she has long since recognized that the way to prosperity lies with clients' long-term interests, and by serving them the independent planner has created strong bonds with a core clientele. Financial services companies which base their marketing strategies on prying clients away from these carefully cultivated relationships will undoubtedly be sorely disappointed.

In competing for new clients with national financial services companies it might appear that the independent is working at a disadvantage. But even though he or she is small and almost invariably lacks significant capital, he or she is also tough and resourceful. If the planner has carefully chosen a broker dealer, there is a strong organization behind him or her. Technological development of support tools for analysis, plan creation, and practice management have freed more and more time for the personal interface activity (i.e., marketing and handholding) at which he or she excels.

The independent planner continues to have the advantage over most major financial services companies of understanding what financial planning is. Large companies, by and large, continue to view their entrances into the field as interesting experiments and frequently managers of these efforts must get in line for attention from decision makers in their companies. The independent, on the other hand, is not only fast and flexible, but also believes wholeheartedly in what he or she does for a living — an attribute that has always helped entrepreneurs in this country.

A prime example of what independents can accomplish lies in the expansion of the corporate executive market, where personal financial planning has been the fastest growing paid perquisite over the past five years. Other than Big Eight accounting firms providing what they call "planning" to executives (primarily of audit clients), and planning units at a few major banks like U.S. Trust, Continental, and BankAmerica, independent planning boutiques have virtual control of this entire segment of the industry. Two of these firms are now owned by financial services giants (Spoor Behrins Campbell & Young by First Interstate and Ayco by American Express), but the sales agreements in both cases specify that the planning companies will be able to pursue their business unhindered by corporate considerations and pressure to sell products manufactured by other corporate subsidiaries. It's uncertain how long that will continue. Two other firms worth mentioning here are Asset Management Group of Denver, the largest remaining independent, and recently beefed up Huggins Financial Services, a division of The Hay Group, the world's largest compensation consulting firm. These firms all offer tax and legal expertise as well as sophisticated investment analysis and the ability to service executives anywhere in the country: a combination that will make it very difficult for new competitors to penetrate this extremely attractive market.

Major Banks

RIHT Financial, a $2.3 billion Providence, Rhode Island bank began offering financial planning through its 115-year-old trust department in 1979. "We quickly saw," says Lawrence G. Knowles, vice president, "that financial planning melded beautifully with the estate planning capability we already had." Three years later, when RIHT began looking at opening a private banking division, it was natural to expand the planning operation and hook it onto The Private Bank, as the division came to be called when it opened its doors in early 1983. "We didn't and don't view planning as a profit opportunity," says Knowles, who manages The Private Bank.

The point of financial planning at RIHT is much the same as at many of the nation's approximately 200 other major banks which control better than 90 percent of the banking system's assets. In reaction to suddenly increased competition in recent years by brokerage firms, financial supermarkets, and other financial services companies, these large institutions first discovered relationship banking, and now with financial planning they have found a way to make this amorphous concept go. Few major banks anywhere are not offering or seriously considering a financial planning service: to establish strong ties with customers, to generate fee income through the sale of additional bank services, and increasingly to earn "commissions" from the sale of non-traditional bank products like tax shelters and mutual funds.

Next to CPAs, bankers consistently earn the highest public confidence ratings in marketing surveys. This plus their ready access to massive numbers of customers represent large banks' main strengths in the financial planning market. Compared with CPAs, independent planners, and smaller banks, large depository institutions also have the resources required to start their own planning departments and mount introductory marketing campaigns.

In New York, for example, Chemical, and more recently, Manufacturers Hanover, have spent hundreds of thousands of dollars over the past few years researching and marketing their retail financial planning services. In the Southeast, NCNB, the region's largest bank, spent heavily to build its Wealthbuilder program, and began rolling it out across North Carolina in 1985. The demand for service has outstripped the bank's planning resources and much of the analytical work on customers' finances is being contracted out to a fee-only independent planning firm. Wealthbuilder will probably be expanded to NCNB's Florida operations in 1986. One more example: Out West, and throughout the country, wherever $9.5 billion First Nationwide Savings has a franchised thrift, this huge collection of S&Ls offer computerized financial planning services to retail bank customers.

In addition, our mid-1985 survey of major banks around the country turned up many more instances of financial planning programs in various stages of development. Portland's $7.5 billion U.S. Bancorp was running a pilot planning program in connection with its Financial Services Account. $45 billion First Interstate was experimenting with a service called Financial Directions in its Colorado banks and planned to spread this private banking oriented planning service to its units throughout the West. In Washington D.C., $4 billion American Security was rolling out an internally built program and Suburban Bancorp in Bethesda was talking with potential joint venture partners.

Commercial loan officers at super giant Chase Manhattan had been selling that bank's upscale planning services to corporate executives for over a year, and its retail division was investigating methods to deliver planning to lower income groups. Bank of Boston, despite its troubles with cash deposits, was moving ahead with its Quisset program, a $495 computerized plan, in one of the most competitive planning markets in the country. Meanwhile, out in the heartland, Cleveland's $6 billion Society Corp. had been getting excellent results through its two-year-old joint venture with Investment Advisors International (a private fee-only firm). Continental Illinois, not burdened with a branch system in its unit banking state, was looking at ways to deliver financial planning electronically to the mass market through ATMs (automatic teller machines). And $4.2 billion United Banks of Colorado had joined with the local office of CIGNA Individual Financial Services to offer financial planning to its upscale customers.

Not all major banks have entered this business, of course. Some are still carefully looking and pondering; others have decided to stay out, at least for the present.

Take giant First Chicago, for example, now the Midwest's largest bank. As long ago as 1982 its retail division conducted a 6-month study of planning as both a product and a marketing vehicle for its high-end customer base of 10,000 Fortune 500 executives. The conclusion may have seemed obvious, but it wasn't.

Richard C. Hartnack, senior vice president financial services, lists three reasons why the "Morgan Guaranty of the Midwest" decided to stay out of the comprehensive planning business. "First," he says, "we concluded that comprehensive planning was not a major revenue opportunity because we would be competing against established independent planners and major accounting firms. These people know the business, whereas we would have been starting from scratch. Second, we determined that planning was not a major marketing opportunity. Our high net worth customers either already had access to planning through their employers or could easily have paid for planning if they had wanted to. Third, a planning department did not appear to offer any long term economic advantage. Our conversations with other banks led us to believe that only a few in unique circumstances [underserved market segments and lack of competition] can make money by offering this service."

Ironically, the in-depth analysis that kept First Chicago out of planning created a strong belief among its officers in the value of broad-based, multidisciplinary planning knowledge, and this in turn led to the bank's relationship manager program. By the end of 1984 more than 100 First Chicago officers had earned or were working toward their CFP designations with the College for Financial Planning. Executives believe this training allows retail officers to better serve customers, by having the ability to give thoughtful, knowledgeable answers to pointed questions about financial planning concerns. Even more noteworthy, First Chicago has not entirely abandoned the planning field. According to Hartnack, in 1984 the bank's retail division began looking at computerized planning as a low-cost marketing tool in the $25,000 to $60,000 income market. "It can't stand up on relative profitability," he says, "but it might well be the toaster of the 1980s."

Indeed, the determination of what type of planning to offer to which market segment is a puzzle for many bankers, and despite the pressure of customer demand and growing competition more than one large institution has proceeded cautiously with its entrance into the business. This care makes sense, for no group of financial services companies, except perhaps accounting firms, has more to lose by falling on their faces than bankers. To make sure they retain customers' trust, most major banks thinking about introducing financial planning have explored every option in an attempt to produce quality service on their first trip out of the gate. Detroit's $14 billion NBD Corp., for example, mounted an exhaustive 18-month investigation. Assistant vice president Willetta Heising and her team looked at most available automated plans, ran private banking clients through some of them, commissioned focus groups, explored joint ventures with Big Eight accounting firms, and talked with a local university about establishing internal training programs. The conclusion: No delivery system works for more than one market segment, and quite possibly each segment needs more than one. "We identified various groups defined by what they wanted in a plan," says Heising, "but pinning down one or two methods that will reach all the members of our target market [private banking customers] has been difficult. The affluent market is truly diverse."

Whether decision makers at more conservative major banks will enter financial planning as aggressively as pioneers like Bank of

America, Chemical, and Security Pacific remains to be seen, of course, but unquestionably bankers are beginning to wake up to the need for powerful, quality marketing in a suddenly more competitive, deregulated environment.

During 1984 and 1985, conferences about financial planning drew increasingly heavy attendance from large banks, just one indication that a growing number perceive the potential marketing applications of financial planning and are anxious to introduce this service in their institutions. In our conversations with executives at large banks across the country we detect increasing willingness to try out new ideas and launch programs before they've been proven to be a sure thing.

At $7 billion CBT in Hartford, for example, when executives were unable to determine, even after months of research, exactly how to launch financial planning for their private banking and personal banking customers, they approved a field test of several methods in early 1985. "We recognized that planning is the cornerstone to present financial services," says senior vice president Sandra Bender, "not a separate profit center or a standalone service. But we weren't certain what the service should look like to meet our customers' needs."

Planning experiments by other major banks have produced some surprising results, and helped these banks tailor their eventual planning programs. At New York's Chemical, for instance, a 1984 joint venture with Integrated Resources, one of the nation's largest NASD broker dealers and a longtime Chemical corporate customer, turned some of the marketing department's "solid" assumptions inside out. For one thing, it rapidly became clear that having a planner in the bank was not important.

Once customers received a direct mail letter from Chemical endorsing Integrated's planning service, and attended a general financial planning seminar at the branch (designed to sell an appointment), it became obvious that a majority wanted to see planners at home or in their offices. Another surprise was the large number of high net worth people attracted to the program, which was deliberately aimed at the retail middle market, defined by Chemical as $30,000 to $70,000 household income. Fully 30 percent had net worths of more than $1 million, and planners wound up, unanticipatedly, referring many customers to Chemical's trust department and other high roller services. Many of these millionaires, it turned out, were on their second or third time through financial planning and showed up enthusiastic and relieved that their trusted bank was finally going to offer them objective service.

Overall, Integrated referred 57 percent of the group who went through the computerized planning process back to Chemical for everything from auto loans to safe deposit boxes. Some mistakes were made, like attempting to attract customers with hefty checking balances (they produced the lowest response), and failing to charge a fee for planning so that customers could walk out comfortably if they chose to implement elsewhere. But what Chemical learned by running this test probably made the difference between success and failure in its current program.

What seems clear in all of these experiments by major banks is a growing recognition among their executives that if they're going to survive, the traditional attitudes and methods of banking are no longer appropriate. A few bank marketing executives with longer experience in financial planning than most of their counterparts have even begun to use the power of this process as an internal marketing tool in their organizations. Perhaps the best example is Craig Madsen, who moved in 1984 from Security Pacific to Wells Fargo, which had gotten out of the planning business in the late 1970s largely because management wanted to avoid the liability problems other bank planning services had run into by matching up clients with private direct investments. With ten years of bank planning experience, Madsen well understands that expertise is the core of the process, but he also knows how difficult it is to make a comprehensive planning service pay.

As a result of his experience, Madsen isn't leading Wells back into the business. Customers who want planning are referred to the fee-only Private Financial Counseling Group in Los Angeles. Shortly after arriving at Wells, Madsen set up a four-day course for employees from trust, private banking, marketing, and the personal investment division. "You can collect all the information you want, but you can't help a customer unless you know how to use it," he says. Employees learn the analytical planning method and how to use microcomputer planning software. Bank customers never see the five-year projections and set of schedules it churns out, but officers use this degraded data to identify customer needs. In addition to being introduced to this planning-derived sales approach, seminar attendees learn how products and services of other Wells divisions can fit into the process to help their customers. The bank already has about 25 CFPs in its various personal financial services divisions. Madsen believes that Wells has begun to change the skills it seeks in hiring.

One other example of breaking with tradition is the way NCNB has marketed its Wealthbuilder program. Not only does the brochure take a shot at "biased planners," clearly pretty aggressive language, but the bank has held tax shelter seminars and set up relationships with selected syndicators to allow full implementation of customers' Wealthbuilder plans.

"The secret to making financial planning go in a bank is understanding marketing and sales," advises Charles Nesbitt, NCNB's senior vice president, financial planning. "Keep them entertained, and they'll remember. Financial affairs don't have to be dull." That's why Nesbitt picked the Quissett plan as the basic building block of the Wealthbuilder program. "Communication is all important in establishing a good relationship," he says. "I like Quissett because it is personable, mildly humorous, and easy to understand."

Market research showed little resistance to Quissett's $495 price, nor to higher fees for the more in-depth diagnosis of Wealthbuilder II, and the fully customized plan, Wealthbuilder III, which runs from $2500 to $3000. Planners in a separate division of NCNB's private bank determine what level customers need based on simple mail-in questionnaires, often filled out by branch officers. Matching the depth of planning to client incomes and net worths should produce satisfied customers, but what Nesbitt really counts on to make his program go, and he believes it will be profitable, is the freedom to be aggressive.

The problem with being tentative with financial planning, Nesbitt and other marketing officers are coming to realize, is potential organizational chaos as ambitious branch managers and personal trust officers set up their own arrangements to satisfy customers' demand for planning, or become increasingly frustrated with their institutions' failure to deliver. "Our retail people want something to help them compete," says one Midwestern bank marketing executive. "They read about financial planning and retirement planning every day, and they know they're missing opportunities. Watching deposits walk out the door to other suppliers has to be frustrating."

Besides keeping their institutions competitive, many officers at large banks are finding that other benefits accrue from planning programs. Private banking units, for example, whose operations formerly suffered from competition between lending and trust officers, have discovered that financial planning can act as a peacemaker, provided planners are given the power to decide what bank services their clients need. It is not, however, a foregone conclusion that major banks will dominate their local markets. Perhaps even more so than community banks, large institutions suffer from a lack of personnel qualified to offer financial planning, and many have had to make difficult changes in salary structures in order to accommodate planners hired from outside. Only a small number of individuals possess the combination of planning expertise and the desire to work within a depository institution, and salaries for competent bank planners have moved up rapidly in recent years as demand outstripped supply.

Large banks are perhaps more vulnerable to losing planners, if only because the large bank environment typically provides more experience and opportunity. Financial planning is an entrepreneurial profession, and long experience at banks like Continental Illinois, which has maintained a trust department financial planning unit since 1971, clearly shows that even very well compensated individuals tend to depart once they recognize the opportunities that await them in private practice.

For most large banks, planning is still an unfamiliar and risky game where the simple demographic rules of checking accounts and CDs don't apply. Quite clearly, in order to succeed against other financial services companies, bank executives need to change their mental set, from marketing makeables to making marketables. So fundamental a change, from contentedly providing transaction services to aggressively seeking out opportunity while fighting off a host of new competitors, is necesary for banks everywhere and of all sizes to survive in a deregulated environment.

With their government granted monopolies suddenly gone, the nation's largest depository institutions are struggling to become competitive marketing organizations. The more progressive institutions realize that instituting a financial planning program, or at least an awareness of planning principles among customer service people, may be the best way to go.

The day will come, predicts Tim Kochis of Bank of America,

when financial planning will achieve the status of a utility. "People will pay for advice monthly, just like electricity or gas," he says. With their established transmission lines and blocks of customers, major banks could easily become the financial services generating plants of the future.

Conclusion

Faced with the type of competition we have catalogued in this chapter, the average community banker may well be wondering if his or her institution has any hope of using financial planning to corner a small share of the market. The financial services giants have a head start, but some reflection should lead readers to the conclusion that they have a much longer course to run. Small banks can get into planning very rapidly, either by using one of the turnkey systems currently being sold by the likes of Bankers Systems or by teaming up with an outside planner in a joint venture arrangement. (See Appendix VI, Case Studies 1-5.)

We do not believe, and almost every market research study we've examined backs us up, that the market for financial planning is anywhere near maturity. As of 1985, only the top 5 percent or so of the population understood what financial planning is and what it can do for their lives. We predict at least five tumultuous years will elapse before the population at large acquires any significant degree of financial sophistication. During that period any player in the industry will have the opportunity to wrap up all the relationships it can establish. Obviously the best way to do just that (why else all the activity?) is by offering true, conscientiously performed financial planning services.

Looking at the immediate future from the supply side, we find more basis for our argument that the window of opportunity in financial services still appears to be wide open. Why do people seek out a financial planner? We believe, and know of no reason to believe otherwise, that they do so when they need help. And people need help only when they have a problem. A new job, a marriage, a divorce, a cross country move, a death, a large inheritance, a large tax assessment, retirement, children soon to enter college — these are all problems. Market research indicates that most Americans run into one of them approximately every five years.

Today, and for the rest of the 1980s as their sophistication grows, fewer and fewer Americans will settle for half-baked solutions. Some seers even argue that by 1990 hardly any financial products and services will be sold outside the context of a financial plan. The opportunity to capture anyone with a problem — and all of their financial resources — clearly exists. But to do so financial services companies must first let the public know that they can help them, and second, actually help them when they walk in the door. In more ways than one, this high stakes marketing and service war has only begun.

5

The Legal and Regulatory Matrix

It is my opinion that the Glass-Steagall Act does not prohibit the Bank from offering investment advice separate from or in conjunction with the brokerage services currently offered by another bank subsidiary.

C. Todd Conover
former Comptroller of the Currency Decision
letter, 9/6/83

Financial Planning Boundaries

If it is done correctly, the financial planning service crosses many of the traditional boundaries that have segmented the financial services marketplace. In fact, this is the source of its strength in the marketplace. Instead of settling for piecemeal services, the consumer can go to one place for investment and tax planning, for advice on insurance, wills, and trusts and, in many cases, shop for investment products as well. More importantly, each financial need is weighed in the context of all the others.

Unfortunately, from the financial planning department's point of view, the consumer's convenience comes at rather a high cost. The regulatory matrix that a lending institution must negotiate to offer all these services is not a simple one. In fact, the most-often cited reason why banks and thrifts have not moved more aggressively into the financial planning marketplace is confusion over what can and cannot be done according to the state banking commissioner, the Federal Deposit Insurance Corp. (FDIC) and Federal Savings and Loan Insurance Company (FSLIC), the Comptroller of the Currency, the Federal Home Loan Bank Board (FHLBB), the Federal Reserve Board, the Securities and Exchange Commission (SEC), and the state securities and insurance commissioners.

Can a bank executive who is not a member of the trust department offer investment advice to banking clients? Can he or she refer clients to an in-house discount brokerage operation with that advice? Can a savings and loan association joint venture directly with a local investment advisor? If so, should the new entity register with the FHLBB, the SEC, both, or neither? What investment products can the bank offer, other than the money market accounts and certificates of deposits (CDs) that are currently on the shelf?

It is not our intention to answer these questions with legal authority, but rather to serve as a guide for establishing the legal marriage of banking and financial planning. Much of this information will be superfluous if the smaller lending institution is able to retain an attorney with experience in banking law and the rather larger field of securities law. Most will find that highly specialized cross-industry practices are still somewhat rare, and they can be very expensive. Recently, a California-based financial services firm called Equitec decided to create a complex investment services menu through its newly-chartered lending institution. To accomplish this, the company hired C. Todd Conover — right out of his former position as the U.S. government's Comptroller of the Currency.

Will it be possible to offer the financial planning service at all, under Glass-Steagall restrictions? Aren't depository institutions prohibited from offering the kind of securities services that are such an important part of financial planning? Five years ago, the answer would have been an unqualified *yes*. Today, the world of banking, securities, and investment manufacturing are inextricably mixed, and growing more so every day. Presently, more than 300 banks offer brokerage services, and soon the number of brokerage accounts opened through banks should be greater than those opened through New York Stock Exchange-registered brokerage houses.

At the same time, the list of companies that operate lending institutions reads like a Who's Who of Wall Street. E.F. Hutton owns a bank in Wilmington, Delaware, Prudential-Bache owns one in Hapeville, Georgia. Shearson/American Express has owned a Seattle-based bank for more than 15 years, and the company's purchase of Minneapolis-based Investors Diversified Services (IDS) brought in a Minneapolis trust company as well. Bear Stearns & Co. in New York owns a bank in Trenton, New Jersey, a few miles south of Drexel Burnham Lambert's bank in Paramus. Banks are owned by the Philadelphia, Midwest, and Pacific Coast Stock Exchanges, by labor unions in Colorado, Kansas, Minnesota, and New York, by Sears, R.H. Macy & Co., Chrysler, Gulf & Western, the 3-M Company, McMahan Valley Stores in Carlsbad, California, and J.C. Penney & Co. Even companies that manufacture investment products have gotten into the act: Integrated Resources, one of the nation's largest manufacturers of tax-sheltered investments, operates a trust company in Colorado. It is joined by such well-known insurance and investment firms as Travelers Corp., Fidelity, Dreyfus, J. & W. Seligman, Keystone, the Vanguard Group, and Wellington Management Company.

Investment Advisers Act of 1940

In fact, if we look at the actual language of the law, and some recent court and regulatory rulings, the environment and its opportunities become somewhat clearer. In the securities field, financial planning is legally defined by the Investment Advisers Act of 1940. According to Section 202(a)(11) of the Act, an investment advisor is defined as any person who, for compensation, engages in the business of advising others, either directly or through publications or writings, as to the value of securities or as to the advisability of investing in, purchasing or selling securities or who, for compensation and as part of a regular business, issues or promulgates analysis or reports concerning securities. This definition specifically excludes banks, or any bank holding company as defined in the Bank Holding Company Act of 1956, which is not an investment company. The statute also exempts lawyers, accountants, engineers, teachers, brokers, dealers, publishers of bona fide newspapers, news magazines, or business or financial publications of general and regular circulation, although the SEC has decided to adopt very narrow definitions of these categories. (Although the words "Savings and Loan Association" are not mentioned anywhere in the Act, an exclusion, under the same terms and conditions, was granted by the Securities and Exchange Commission in a July, 1982 no-action letter.)

Glass-Steagall Act of 1933

In the banking industry, the relationship between banking and securities activities is the Glass-Steagall Act of 1933 (48 Stat. 184) — a bill that was passed in the shadow of some of the banking industry's more flagrant excesses prior to the Great Depression. The Act has since been codified in various sections of 12 U.S.C. Sec. 24, 78, 335, 377 and 378, and represents an attempt to balance the benefits that banks provided against the hazards and financial dangers that arise when banks engage in certain outside activities. In its 1971 ruling in the case of *Investment Company Institute* vs *Camp* (401 US 617), the U.S. Supreme Court outlined these as follows:

1. The danger that banks might invest their own assets in imprudent stock;
2. The tendency of promotional pressures to force banks to make unsound loans or extend assistance to an affiliate engaged in securities activities;

3. The danger of loss of public confidence in a bank, if the securities affiliate fared poorly;

4. Potential loss to bank depositors on investments they had purchased on reliance upon the relationship between the bank and its securities affiliate;

5. The danger that a bank's reputation for prudence and restraint would be undercut by risks involved in investment banking;

6. The danger that banks might make loans to customers to facilitate the purchase of securities promoted by a securities affiliate;

7. The conflict between a bank's "salesman's stake" and its obligation to render disinterested investment advice;

8. The danger that a bank's securities affiliate would unload excessive or unproductive holdings on bank trust customers.

To prevent these potential abuses, the drafters of the Act included four different sections which addressed the relationship between banking and securities activities. Section 16 restricts the securities activities of national banks by prohibiting them from underwriting any issue of securities or stock. It authorizes national banks to purchase for their own accounts only U.S. Treasury obligations, obligations of specified federal government agencies, and general obligations of states and municipalities. (Both Section 5(c) and portions of the Federal Reserve Act broaden this restriction so that it also applies to the state chartered banks which are members of the Federal Reserve system.) The "salesman's stake" and "unloading" issues are specifically addressed as follows:

> "The business of dealing in securities and stock by [national banks] shall be limited to purchasing and selling such securities and stock without recourse solely upon the order and for the account of customers, and in no case for its own account, and the association will not underwrite any issue of securities or stock: provided that the association may purchase for its own account investment securities under such limitations and restrictions as the Comptroller of the Currency may by regulation prescribe."

There follows a rather lengthy list of exceptions which, among other things, permits banks to underwrite and deal in various government securities, but these have little relevance to a bank's retail securities activities.

Section 21 of the Glass-Steagall Act addresses the same concerns in reverse, barring securities firms from engaging in banking activities. By strong implication, however, it effectively brings all banks under the Section 21 restrictions, broadening the Section 16 prohibitions beyond national banks and state member banks to any entity engaged "to any extent in the business of receiving deposits subject to check or to repayment upon presentation of a passbook, certificate of deposit or other evidence of debt, or upon request of the depositor." The wording goes on to bar any person or organization engaged in the business of issuing, underwriting, selling or distributing stocks, bonds, debentures, notes or other securities at wholesale or retail, or through syndicate participation, from also engaging in any of the aforementioned depository banking activities. In *Board of Governors of Federal Reserve System* vs *Investment Company Institute* (450 US 46, 63; 1981), the Court commented that this section was intended to make doubly certain that the connections between "securities firms, such as underwriters or brokerage houses" and depository institutions were thoroughly severed.

Sections 20 and 32 of the Act prohibit affiliations between banks and securities organizations, although they are stated in somewhat different terms than the Section 16 and 21 prohibitions that apply directly to banking activities. Section 20 provides that no national or member bank may be "affiliated" with any corporation, association, business trust, or other similar organization engaged principally in the issuance, flotation, underwriting, public sale, or distribution at wholesale or retail, or through syndicate participation of stocks, bonds, debentures, notes or other securities. The term "affiliate" is rather broadly defined to include any corporation, business trust, association, or similar organization which the bank directly or indirectly owns, or which it controls with more than 50 percent of the number of shares voted. Although "affiliate" as originally defined in Section 2(b) of the Glass-Steagall Act did not include holding companies, Congress in 1966 amended the statute to bring holding companies within the definition of "affiliate," and thereby within the reach of Section 20 (80 Stat. 242, 12 U.S.C. Section 22a(b)(4).

Section 32 (12 U.S.C. Section 377), on the other hand, prevents the sharing of personnel between national and member banks and securities firms. It prohibits any officer, director, employee, or partner of any Federal Reserve system member bank from serving at the same time as an officer, director, or employee of any firm "primarily engaged in the issue, floatation, underwriting, public sale or distribution at wholesale or retail . . . of stocks, bonds or similar securities."

A careful reading will uncover three potentially significant distinctions between the affiliation prohibitions of Sections 20 and 32 and the bank prohibitions outlined in Sections 16 and 21. First of all, the bank prohibitions apply to all banks — and, under the SEC's more recent no-action letter, to savings and loan associations as well. The affiliation prohibitions, on the other hand, are worded so as to only apply to banks which are members of the Federal Reserve system. This distinction alone would appear to open the door to full securities activities for all non-member banks and savings and loan associations.

Second, the bank prohibitions outlined in Sections 16 and 21 expressly permit certain securities brokerage activities; specifically, those purchases and sales which take place solely upon the order and for the account of customers. In Sections 20 and 32, the only language that could be interpreted to refer to brokerage activities is a prohibition relating to "public sale" of securities. If this can be construed to refer, not to the underwriting activities which the remainder of the Section deals with, but rather to sales by an agent for the seller, then these activities would be prohibited under the Glass-Steagall Act. If it refers to purchase and sales of securities, as would appear more likely from the context, then there is no restriction.

Finally, the affiliation prohibitions contained in Sections 20 and 32 apply only to securities firms which engage *principally* or *primarily* in the listed securities activities. The Act never refers to investment advice or implies that it belongs on the listing of prohibited activities. From this, it appears that a lending institution that wishes to offer financial planning services could enter into a direct relationship with any primarily fee-based local planning firms. In the case where a planning firm is divided into an investment advisory arm and a broker-dealer or sales arm — a situation which is relatively common in the financial planning marketplace — the lending institution might be able to legally enter into a relationship with the advisory arm, which would refer business directly to the sales arm under some sort of shared arrangement.

Legal Precedent

Although relatively few lending institutions have attempted to take advantage of the potential opportunities that are implicit in the language of the Glass-Steagall Act, their pioneering efforts have been tested and upheld in the courts.

In the Supreme Court's 1981 *Board of Governors* decision, for example, the Court went so far as to suggest that the performance of investment advisory services to a closed-end mutual fund by a bank would not necessarily violate Section 16 or 21 of the Glass-Steagall Act — a ruling which clearly opens the door to managing discretionary accounts outside of the trust department. Even if it were assumed a bank would violate the Act by engaging in certain investment advisory activities, it did not necessarily follow that a bank holding company's nonbank affiliate could never perform those services. The Court concluded, in part, that "The management of a customer's investment portfolio — even when the manager has the power to sell securities owned by the customer — is not the kind of selling activity that Congress contemplated when it enacted Section 21 . . . [Section 21] surely was not intended to require banks to abandon an accepted banking practice that was subjected to regulation under Section 16."

The conclusion is not difficult to interpret. If the lending institution avoids the kind of selling activity covered by Section 21 — when it has investment discretion and is directing specific portfolio purchases and sales — then there certainly could be no illegal sale of securities where the bank does not have the ultimate investment discretion with respect to a customer's portfolio. As the Court itself noted, the statutory list of activities prohibited to banks — that is, "issuing, underwriting, selling or distributing . . . securities" — is hardly the sort of language that would be used to describe an investment advisor.

What about the liability question implicit in the language of Section 16? This section prohibits a national bank from purchasing and selling securities except where the transaction is "without recourse" to the bank. The Court argued that while the bank might be subject to certain incidental and contingent liabilities based on its role as broker or advisor, these are not the types of recourse Congress appeared to be attempting to bar. Congress, it reasoned, was concerned about the sort of contractual arrangements that would effectively put a bank in the shoes of the investor, subject to the risks ordinarily associated with any particular investment. In this vein, the Supreme Court described the "without recourse" wording as being directed against contracts "by which the bank assumes the risk of loss which would otherwise fall on the buyer of securities, or undertakes to insure to the seller the benefit of an increase in value of securities which would otherwise accrue to the bank."

In Footnote 24 of the ruling, the Court went on to state:

> *Section 21 prohibits firms engaged in the securities business from also receiving deposits. Bank holding companies do not receive deposits and the language of Section 21 cannot be read to include within its prohibition certain organizations related by ownership with a bank, which does receive deposits.*

If this interpretation of the federal laws continues to govern securities and banking activities, then it appears that virtually all lending institutions are empowered to provide investment advice and some retail securities services. The important question then becomes, not "Can I?" but "How should I?" Structurally and methodologically, in what ways can a lending institution offer financial planning to its customers, and how does the structure affect the all-important regulatory considerations?

From a regulatory standpoint, there are three basic ways such a service can be established — in-house, joint ventures, or rental agreements. Each places the bank under a different group of federal watchdogs and within different legal constraints.

In-House Planning

The first option would place the service "in house." Providing investment advice has historically been recognized as a banking service, which has been provided either through personal contact or through impersonal subscription services. A number of court cases have upheld this view, including *United States* vs *Philadelphia National Bank* (374 U.S. 321, 326-27 n.5; 1963), *United States* vs *Idaho First National Bank* (315 F. Supp. 261, 273-74; 1970), *United States* vs *First National Bank of Maryland* (310 F. Supp. 157, 163 n.7, 173; 1970), *United States* vs *Third National Bank in Nashville* (Trade Cases; CCH). (The attorney who wishes to further establish the point can also obtain rather lengthy studies by the SEC and the Senate Committee on Banking, Housing, and Urban Affairs.)

What is less clear is the lending institution's ability to integrate the investment advisor activities that have been traditionally offered through trust departments with the implementation phase of financial planning — specifically, with implementation that involves the actual recommendation or purchase of specific investments.

If the bank has a trust department, the financial planning service could be simply inserted there, either as an ancillary service or as the organizing principle of all the various fee-based activities that it currently offers. Interestingly enough, although this is where financial planning services have traditionally been offered by the banking community, it is also the most limited in terms of financial plan implementation. How?

There is a well-worn rule that trustees may not profit from the administration of a trust except for the receipt of compensation for service as trustee. That means that the sale of broker-dealer services may be made to a trust account, but this can only be done if no commission is charged to the trust accounts — a circumstance which removes a great deal of the incentive to provide the service. The precedent for this view includes a 1927 British case (*Williams* vs *Barton*) in which a trustee directed trust securities transactions to a brokerage firm where he was employed, and received a percentage of the brokerage commissions in return. The court found the trustee accountable to the trust for his portion of the commissions. This position was supported in *Sexton* vs *Swords S.S. Line, Inc.* (118 F 2d 708; 2nd Cir. 1941), *Slay* vs *Burnett Trust* (143 Tex 621, 187 S.W. 2d 480), and in a decision of the Comptroller of the Currency to charter Dreyfus National Bank and Trust Company.

For state-chartered non-member banks and those that are members of the Federal Reserve system, the trust department may offer the only permissible in-house connection with brokerage (plan implementation) activities. An opinion of the FDIC General Counsel, dated May 23, 1983, concludes that investment advice may not be offered, since it is outside the traditional role of banks — with the exception of trust departments. On August 11, 1983, when the Federal Reserve Board revised Regulation Y to add discount brokerage as a pre-approved activity for bank holding companies, it specifically conditioned the pre-approved decision upon the absence of investment advice connected with the brokerage service. For those institutions that fall directly under the FDIC and Federal Reserve Board's supervision, one of the non-in-house options might be preferred.

For national banks and savings and loan associations, the lending institution interested in offering financial planning services would establish a retail banking division within its current organizational framework, whose staff's mission would be to offer additional fee-based services to the bank's most valued customers. This could be done most quickly and easily either by hiring a financial planning professional on a salary, rather than a commission or combination basis, or by entering into a contractual agreement with one of several "turn key" financial planning vendors that now work with banks.

If the former route is chosen, the in-house planner would be responsible for evaluation and analysis, and could cross refer high-net-worth clients to other banking services in the course of plan implementation. The bank could also establish a discount brokerage service, in order to position itself to receive more of the "implementation" business, and it could contract out for due diligence analyses from a number of companies that now research the limited partnership market on behalf of banks and lending institutions.

Working with a "turn key" vendor, on the other hand, offers the advantages of having the client contacts handled by personnel who are already members of the banking staff, who would receive some form of training in interview techniques and data gathering. The information might be sent away for computerized analysis, and return with specific recommendations that could be explained in detail by bank personnel. Some of these planning firms have gone so far as to create customized investment products for the clients of lending institutions — a market that appears certain to grow in the near future.

Under each of these "in-house" scenarios, the company would

enjoy a statutory exemption from regulation by the SEC under the Investment Advisers Act of 1940, and from the somewhat complex reporting requirements that SEC regulation entails.

Since January 1, however, the lending institution may find itself under several sets of regulations at once, answering to the Comptroller's office, the Federal Reserve Board or the Federal Home Loan Bank Board, to the federal insurer, and to the SEC under powers it granted itself back in July of 1985. Release Number 22205 effectively cancelled the regulatory exemptions for banking institutions contained in Sections 3(a) (4) and 3(a) (5) of the Securities Exchange Act of 1934, adding in its place Rule 3b-9, which provides that an exemption shall not apply to any bank which 1) publicly solicits brokerage business either on or off the bank's premises; 2) receives transaction-related compensation for accounts on which the bank provides advice; or 3) deals in or underwrites securities.

There are, however, some exceptions specified in the new rule. Banks which have entered into "networking" arrangements, and which send customers to a broker-dealer under some form of revenue-sharing arrangement, are exempted so long as the broker-dealer is clearly identified as the entity performing the brokerage services, the bank employees receive no compensation for the brokerage activities, and perform only clerical and ministerial functions in connection with them. Banks with fewer than 1,000 transactions per year are also exempted, and there is a provision which appears to exempt securities transactions on behalf of money market or other collectively managed funds, where investors' assets are pooled and the customer's position is a passive one. At this writing, several lawsuits have been filed which could have the effect of negating SEC regulation of banking activities for some foreseeable time in the future; however this ruling would appear to make it less attractive for the lending institution to create planning capabilities in-house.

Joint Ventures

The second structural option that is open to lending institutions for their financial planning departments lies in somewhat better-charted regulatory waters. Rather than taking an in-house approach, the company would apply to the Federal Reserve Board under Regulation Y for permission to establish a nonbanking subsidiary of a bank holding company (BHC) — a routine procedure with no ongoing regulation involved. The BHC can have either a discount brokerage subsidiary and a financial planning subsidiary, but the two must be distinctly separate. The separate entity would offer the financial planning service with some degree of cooperation with the parent company. Generally this is accomplished through cross-referrals and by having the planner's office facing the high-traffic area of the banking lobby.

In a section of the Garn-St Germain Depository Institutions Act of 1982 known as the Banking Affiliates Act of 1982, the U.S. Congress amended the Federal Reserve Act (12 U.S.C. 371c) to more clearly specify the general rules governing the affiliates of lending institutions. In general, the language of the Act states that a covered transaction between a bank and an affiliate can take place only if the aggregate amount of covered transactions of the member bank and its subsidiaries does not exceed 10 percent of the capital stock and surplus of the member bank. In the case of all affiliates, the total amount of such transactions may not exceed 20 percent of the same figure. Certainly, these are not likely to become onerous restrictions, but they should be kept in mind when structuring a new company affiliate. The definition of an affiliate is set forth in the following language:

(A) any company that controls the member bank and any other company that is controlled by the company that controls the member bank,

(B) a bank subsidiary of the member bank,

(C) any company —

(i) that is controlled directly or indirectly, by a trust or otherwise, by and for the benefit of shareholders who beneficially or otherwise control, directly or indirectly, by trust or otherwise, the member bank or any company that controls the member bank; or

(ii) in which a majority of its directors or trustees constitute a majority of the persons holding any such office with the member bank or any company that controls the member bank;

(D) any investment company with respect to which a member

bank or any affiliate thereof is an investment advisor as defined in section 2(1)(20) of the Investment Company Act of 1940.

Later, the term "covered transaction" is defined to include loans or extension of credits, purchase of or investment in securities, purchase of assets, including assets subject to an agreement to repurchase, the acceptance of securities issued by the affiliate as collateral security for a loan or extension of credit to any person or company or the issuance of a guarantee, acceptance, or letter of credit.

The permissibility of joint venture arrangements in the securities arena appears to be amply supported by recent court rulings. Under Section 32 of the Glass-Steagall Act, banks are prohibited from joint-venturing directly with securities firms or, by strong implication, with the NASD-registered broker-dealers and registered representatives who make up a great majority of the financial planners in the American marketplace.

But what about joint-venturing through a subsidiary of the bank? The U.S. Supreme Court addressed this issue in its 1981 *Board of Governors* decision, referring back to a provision in the Bank Holding Company Act (12 U.S.C. Sections 1841 and 1843(c)(8)) which permits bank holding companies and their nonbank affiliates to conduct activities that are deemed to be so closely related to banking or managing or controlling banks as to qualify as a proper incident to banking. In its decision, the Court held that services provided by investment advisors were not significantly different from the traditional functions of banks, and thus the Federal Reserve Board could probably conclude that investment advisors' activities satisfied the Bank Holding Company standards of being "closely related to banking" and "a proper incident thereto."

In the past 36 months, several of the lending institutions' governing bodies have been called upon to more clearly define the relationship between investment advisory services and their permissible connection with the sales or transfer of securities.

National Banks

On November 4, 1983, the Comptroller approved the application of Security Pacific National Bank to offer discount brokerage services through a newly created bank subsidiary, a decision which was challenged and ultimately upheld by the U.S. Supreme Court. Although this was widely regarded as the beginning of the era of banks offering brokerage activities, and was the first of several suits to reach the High Court, the Office of the Comptroller of the Currency (OCC) had already approved on March 31, 1983, a similar application by American National Bank of Austin, Texas.

On April 6 of the same year, the OCC approved an application which proposed to establish a subsidiary to provide investment advice — to be called MPACT Securities Corp. — which would register with the SEC as an investment advisor and provide individualized advice to clients concerning their investment portfolios. The clients, under the proposal, would either retain the ultimate investment discretion or contract with the advisor to supervise their portfolios. In addition, the subsidiary would generate a fee-supported investment advisory newsletter which would contain recommendations concerning the purchase and sale of specific securities.

As a precedent, most observers feel that the key to the application revolved around the relationship between the discount brokerage operation and the investment advisor. The application indicated that although the two companies would share the MPACT name, there would be no shared employees, nor would the two companies share office space or telephone lines. There would, however, be some referral of customers from the brokerage operation to MPACT Securities and vice versa. In fact, the newsletter would be marketed to customers of MPACT Brokers, and the investment advisor would effect transactions through the brokerage operation to obtain "best execution," although the advisor would obtain the written consent of clients before effecting any such transactions.

Thus, with the OCC's approval, the bank owned and controlled both a discount brokerage and an advisory service under separate subsidiaries. As limitations, the advisor would not share any fees with the broker, nor would the broker share any commissions with the advisor. The advisor would not receive any form of payment for referring advisory clients to the brokers, as this is prohibited by the Advisors Act except as set forth in Rule 206(4)-3 (17 C.F.R. paragraph 275.206(4)-3). There were also some voluntary disclosure restrictions in the application: The broker's portion of the commission would be disclosed to the client whenever such a transaction was effected.

The Comptroller ruled that the statutory test was met if no sales or purchases were executed unless directed by the customer, and the customer has full beneficial ownership of the securities. The opinion went even further and stated that these conditions would be met even if the bank were to offer investment advice incidental to brokerage transactions. Like most financial planners in the marketplace at large, in other words, the client would receive investment advice and analysis (a financial plan), then would have the option to implement it through the planner at hand or through another outlet of his or her choosing.

Regarding the commission structure and its relationship to potential conflicts of interest, however, the Comptroller required the bank to obtain a favorable opinion of counsel prior to retention of full commissions by the broker. This was due to the historical prohibition against banks profiting from trust trading activities. Here, state laws come into play, which may impose additional fiduciary duties.

What can we conclude from this? It appears that for subsidiaries of national banks, an in-house advisory service is now authorized. This advisory service could refer the clients to the in-house discount brokerage services or other brokers for specific product implementation. Of course, the underwriting of securities is still prohibited. It should also be noted that the SEC has begun a campaign to bring bank-operated discount brokerage services under its regulatory authority.

State Non-Member Banks

We have already seen that the FDIC has taken the position that investment advisory services offered in-house through anything other than a trust department is not permissible. But what if such services are offered through some form of subsidiary relationship? In September 1982, the FDIC issued a "Statement of Policy on the Applicability of Insured Non-Member Banks" (News Release PR-72-82; 47 Fed. Reg. 38, 984), which stated, in part:

> The Glass-Steagall Act does not by its terms prohibit an insured non-member bank from establishing an affiliate relationship with, or organizing or acquiring a subsidiary corporation that engages in the business of issuing, underwriting, selling or distributing at whole-

sale or retail, or through syndicate participation, stocks,
bonds, debentures, notes or other securities. While the
Glass-Steagall Act was intended to protect banks from
certain risks inherent in particular securities activities,
it does not reach securities activities of a bona fide sub-
sidiary of an insured non-member bank.

The FDIC went on to issue a proposed rule (Fed. Reg. 42, 121;
September 24, 1982) which would dramatically expand the scope of
securities activities nonmember state depository institutions could
perform. Specifically, it would require, first, that an FDIC-insured,
non-Federal Reserve bank give notice to the FDIC of its intent to invest in a securities subsidiary. Prior approval of the investment by
the FDIC would not be required, however. Second, it would prohibit
an FDIC-insured non-member bank from establishing or acquiring a
subsidiary that underwrites securities (other than activities the bank
itself would be permitted to conduct) unless (a) the underwriting activity is on a "best efforts" basis, is restricted to debt securities with
specified high credit rating or is underwriting of money market-type
mutual funds and (b) the subsidiary is a bona fide subsidiary.

Since then, the FDIC's legal division has issued General Counsel
Opinion No. 6 (Federal Register No., 22989; May 23, 1983), whose
most well-known effect was to put the FDIC's stamp of approval on
bank-offered discount brokerage services. The opinion goes somewhat further, however, allowing the bank to act as a conduit of information to the discount broker-dealer, with the bank confirming
transactions with the customers. The bank could also act as custo-
dian for the customer's securities. In either case, it could receive a
portion of the broker's commission generated by each transaction.

Although the opinion did not specifically comment on all the
various formats of a relationship, it did state that it would not cite
as a violation of the Glass-Steagall Act a program in which:

1. the bank clearly acted solely at the customer's direction;
2. the transactions were made for the account of the customer,
   and not the account of the bank;
3. the transactions were without recourse;
4. the bank makes no warranty as to the performance or quality
   of any security; and

5. the bank did not advise the customer to make any particular investment decision.

The legal division was of the opinion that the bank may lawfully promote discount brokerage services, but must be careful to prevent public misconception about the bank's function with regard to the securities investment. If the bank intends to use the contractual arrangement with the broker-dealer for transactions executed in connection with trust department accounts, the bank should not receive any additional compensation with regard to those transactions from the broker-dealer. In other words, the bank trust department should not share in any commission associated with the transaction. To do so would raise possibilities of a breach of fiduciary obligation toward the bank's trust account customers. If a bank does more than simply introduce bank customers to a broker-dealer pursuant to a contractual arrangement, the bank will be required to maintain additional records.

Thus, for banks and their affiliates controlled by the FDIC (insured non-member banks), it appears that a bona fide subsidiary would be the best vehicle with which to offer financial planning services. The bank itself, or an affiliate, could provide the discount brokerage services. The bank customer should be informed that it is not the bank that is providing the advisory services.

Savings and Loan Associations

Federally-chartered savings and loan associations and federal savings banks are governed by the Home Owners' Loan Act 12 (U.S.C. Sec. 1464), otherwise known as HOLA. In recent years, the scope of authorized activities has been expanded by statute and by regulatory interpretation. The Garn-St. Germain Act (Public Law No. 97-320, 96 Stat. 1469 (1982)) amended HOLA Section 5(a), allowing the FHLBB to charter and regulate federal associations for the purposes of providing for the deposit or investment of funds, the extension of credit for homes and other goods and services. In subparagraph (c)(4)(B), the Act also authorized a federal association to invest in a service corporation. The FHLBB's regulations implementing the service corporation investment authority (12 CFR Section 545.74(c)) require that the activities be authorized by regulation or approved by specific action of the board, and must be limited to activities that are "reasonably related" to the activities of the parent institution.

The FHLBB has been called upon to decide more fully than any other regulatory organization just how closely a discount brokerage operation can be integrated with the day-to-day activities of a lending institution. In separate cases involving Fortune Federal and Poughkeepsie Savings Bank, the savings and loan associations proposed to establish discount brokerage operations where certain employees of the association would register as brokers and serve as part-time salaried employees. In addition, the applications contemplated the presence of registered principals, who would not be employed by the savings and loan association or its service corporation, who would receive the commissions.

Under another application, submitted by First American Federal, a wholly owned service corporation would be permitted to enter into an agreement with a newly-formed discount brokerage operation. The service corporation would earn a percentage of the gross commissions generated from transactions on the customer's account opened by the service corporation. Only mutual funds and debt and equity securities could be traded. No investment advice would be rendered, and all securities transactions would be executed by the brokerage firm after telephone contact with the customer. In each case, the FHLBB approved the application, but recommended that each firm receive opinion of counsel that the brokerage service corporation's internal control and supervisory systems met securities industry standards.

The FHLBB has also issued a ruling which can be considered analogous to the OCC's MPACT Securities letter: It is the most complete definition of what a savings and loan association may and may not do in the area of financial planning and financial plan implementation. On May 6, 1982, the board approved applications permitting service corporations of federal associations to engage in the securities brokerage activities using the services of a corporation known as IN-VEST — an NASD-registered securities broker.

Under the initial application, INVEST proposed to engage in three basic types of activities:

1. Executing purchases and sales of equity securities, municipal securities and public utility bonds for the accounts of others.

2. Providing customers with investment advisory services including portfolio analysis and valuation.

3. Assisting its participating associations in the implementation of the program by offering marketing and training services.

INVEST did not propose to underwrite or sell any issue of stock or securities for its own account, but stated that its representatives would be physically located in the place of business of the association. Although there would be no mutual employees, the association would present literature explaining the INVEST services to customers and introduce customers to its customer representatives. The representatives (typically association employees who have been trained by INVEST and receive a salary from the company) would be registered as brokers and would not receive commissions. They would also not be allowed to recommend any investment or transaction which had not been approved by INVEST's home office.

The company later received approval to set up shop in state-chartered banks, and has embarked on a cautious course toward installing financial planning services that illustrates just how far banks and savings and loan associations can go toward full-service planning for their customers. Smaller net-worth clients, with assets of below $100,000, receive a workbook which guides them through a do-it-yourself financial plan. More substantial banking customers receive a computer-generated plan from the company's Tampa, Florida headquarters. In the implementation stage, customer representatives will often recommend the bank or savings and loan association's in-house investment products, such as CDs or money market accounts.

Thus, it appears that if a savings and loan association wants to establish a department to offer retail financial planning, it is necessary that the company set up and maintain a separate entity from the association itself — along the lines of the INVEST program. This would appear to allow the company to contract with other turn-key vendors or joint venture directly with a local financial planning firm — even to the extent that the lending institution's employees could participate in the marketing and referral (but not sales) processes. The INVEST approval did authorize the service corporation to provide customers with investment advisory services, including portfolio analysis and valuation.

Federal Reserve Member Banks

Of all the banking regulators, the Federal Reserve Board has been the most cautious about expanding the authority of its member banks. Recently, however, it too issued a decision which could have a significant effect on the industry as a whole.

The ruling, dated August 1, 1984, involved an application by New York-based Manufacturers Hanover Corp., which proposed to deal in government securities, state bond obligations, and market instruments, and to offer free investment advice on those securities through a subsidiary corporation called Manufacturers Hanover Money Market Corp. Although these activities were not permitted for the parent company, the Federal Reserve Board ruled that they were permissible in a subsidiary — that is, an entity that would not be subject to interstate branching restrictions. The effect, in the eyes of some observers, is to allow the company to establish a nationwide network of brokerage offices, where commission-based planning could be offered to major corporations and sophisticated "qualified" investors.

From this, it would appear that the establishment of some form of external entity would answer most if not all of the most pressing objections raised by bank and thrift regulators, and which are contained in federal law. The most common structure for a savings and loan association is to set up a joint venture directly with a financial planning firm that is already practicing in the area. Banks, on the other hand, could set up a holding company, which would create a planning subsidiary using the bank's assets much as any other investor might set up a corporation.

In each case, the lending institution typically provides much if not all of the initial capital and access to its customers. The planning firm offers immediate investment sophistication, will often agree to serve clients under the bank's name, and will agree to cross-refer traditional banking services required by the typically high-net-worth customers who are attracted by the service. The fastest, easiest, and least expensive solution may be to directly associate or contract with an independent financial planning firm — which would also lessen Glass-Steagall "affiliation" concerns. This could be done on an exclusive arrangement for the bank's marketing area. The outside firm should not charge its own clients less than the bank charges, and client meetings should take place on the bank's premises so that the service would be more closely identified with the institution.

What about division of fees? The financial planning firm could enter into an arrangement whereby the share of fees is increased according to the growth in the volume of business. For example, one arrangement might give the bank 10 percent of the fees generated by the first 10 customers, 20 percent of the fees from the next 90, and 30 percent of the fees exceeding that. From the planning firm's point of view, this would provide the lending institution partner with a powerful incentive to promote the service vigorously.

If this structure is employed by the lending institution, the new entity falls under regulation by the SEC but not, generally, under the more complex matrix of banking regulation. Of course, the outside planner or turn-key planning firm should be a registered investment advisor pursuant to the Investment Advisers Act, and any contract should make it clear that the bank itself does not intend to hold a salesman's stake in any security that is ultimately recommended for purchase or sale. In addition, an opinion of counsel should be obtained regarding a division or retention of any fees earned from commissions for account transactions — particularly where they involve a trust account.

Rental Agreements

The lending institution's third structual option is probably the simplest of all to implement. Instead of offering financial planning services directly, the company could bring in a planner from the outside, place that person in a banking office off of the main lobby, and charge rental fees based on a preset formula on the volume of business conducted in that office.

A bank in Connecticut currently has such an arrangement with H&R Block, an insurance agent, a travel agent, and INVEST. In 1984, Chemical Bank structured a similar arrangement with Integrated Resources Equity Corp., the broker-dealer arm of the New York-based investment house.

In the sale of life insurance contracts, this kind of arrangement has proved to be a way to circumvent the more-or-less ironclad regulations keeping bankers out of the market. As early as April of 1983, executives at Nationwide Insurance had reached an agreement with Banc One in Columbus, Ohio, whereby fully-commissioned agents were stationed in walled-off sections of the lobbies of two branch offices. Today, the lobby of Banc One's heavily-trafficked suburban Columbus branch includes 1,400 square feet of leased space whose tenants offer brokerage, insurance, real estate, and travel agency services. There are plans to convert nine other units sometime in 1986. American National Bank in California and Boston-based John Hancock Life have conducted an experiment along similar lines, with 40 percent of all sales commissions going to the banks in the form of rent. Bank of America has agents from Liberty National Life stationed in 22 branch offices, where they sell term, universal, and interest-sensitive whole life policies. SAFECO and First Interstate Bancorp have programs set up in 55 branches.

Under federal law (12 U.S.C. 29 and 12 U.S.C. 24 (Seventh)), lending institutions enjoy a well-established right to lease excess office space in bank-owned buildings. This concept was upheld in a number of court cases. The precedents include *Brown* vs *Schleier* (118 F. 981, 984; 8th Circuit, 1902) and *Wingert* vs *First National Bank* (175 F. 739, 741; 4th Circuit, 1909). The most recent case was *Wirtz* vs *First National Bank & Trust Company* (365 F 2d 641, 644; 10th Circuit, 1966), where the 10th Circuit court's decision read, in part: "A recognized incident to building, and to spread its expenses and operating costs by renting space to tenants."

If the concept of banks renting space is legally sound, what about the type of lease that they can offer? Here the question appears to hinge on whether the terms of the lease are similar to those in the general marketplace at large. Percentage leases are relatively common, particularly in shopping malls, and became widespread as early as the Great Depression. The final potential regulatory roadblock lies in the question of whether a bank that is sharing in the insurance or securities commissions generated in its own lobby is actually in the insurance or securities business. Put more generally — is the owner of a shopping mall actively engaged in the business of selling the various products that are offered in the stores on his or her premises? In the banking business, the 5th Circuit Court addressed this question in *Saxon* vs *Georgia Association of Independent*

Insurance Agents (399 F. 2nd 1010; 5th Circuit, 1968), and found that despite the existence of a percentage lease with an insurance agent, the bank in question was not engaging in the insurance business or acting as an insurance agent.

Is it possible that the bank and the insurance agency have formed a tacit partnership under a percentage lease arrangement? Under the Uniform Partnership Act (Section 7(4)(b)), this does not happen in the usual situation — a position that was supported in two cases decided at a time when percentage leases were first becoming accepted in the marketplace (*H.T. Hackney Company* vs *Robert E. Lee Hotel*; 300 S.W. 1 (Tenn. 1927) and *Wagner* vs *Buttles*; 139 NIW. 425 (Wisconsin 1913)). In an aside in the latter decision, the Court noted that only in a case where the percentage required under the lease is unusually high or the lessor exercises management control over the lessee's business would an inference of partnership arise. If the bank contracts on the basis of terms usual and customary in the field of commercial leasing, this situation should not arise. More recently, in *Wright* vs *Trotta* (367 A.2d 557, 561-62; Md. 1976), the Court held that a lease with an insurance agency, on which the rent was based in part on a percentage of gross premiums, did not contravene a state law prohibiting the payment of commissions or fees to unlicensed persons for procuring insurance. *State* vs *Gus Blass Co.* (105 S.W. 2d 853; Ark. 1937) presented a comparable situation, where a department store that leased space to an optometry firm on a percentage basis was held not to be thereby practicing optometry.

Although First Interstate, Chemical, American National, and Bank of America clearly enjoy a kind of tacit approval from the Federal Reserve Board, the only regulatory body to issue a definitive ruling on the net lease concept is the Comptroller of the Currency. In a letter dated December 2, 1983, the Comptroller discussed the relevant portions of an application made on behalf of Miami, Florida-based American Bankers Insurance Group, where the company proposed to lease space in national banks and offer a full range of insurance products to the bank's customers and the general public. Under the proposal, the insurance agent who would market the insurance products would not be an employee of the bank, but rather an independent agent or licensed employee of an insurance agent. This individual would rent space adjacent to the retail banking area, with the terms of the lease calling for rent based on the amount of space used, the volume generated, and the various services provided by the parties to the agreement.

The letter went on to confront the "safety and soundness" question in some detail, noting that such an arrangement can actually prove beneficial to the safety and soundness of the U.S. banking system as a whole:

> *"Many banks today are operating with the substantial financial burden of extensive and expensive branch networks. As banks place greater emphasis on the more efficient and economical delivery of banking services, such as by electronic means, the need to make their "brick and mortar" facilities more profitable increases. The rental by banks of excess space in their branch offices seems to be an appropriate vehicle for alleviating the fixed costs associated with these locations."*

Even so, the Comptroller advised that national bank lessors include a clause in the leasing contract expressly negating a partnership or joint venture and, for safety and soundness purposes, the clause should also preclude any bank liability for the tenant's debts and liabilities. He also warned that the lending institution was obligated to assure that the insurance agency lessor be appropriately and separately identified through the use of signs and proper labelling, concluding that some effort to differentiate the two must be made so that the public will understand that it is not buying insurance from the bank.

Bank advertising and literature that mentions the insurance agency should also make clear the agency's independent ownership and operation. In addition, the relationship between the bank and the insurance agency should be at arms-length. The Comptroller specifically advised against leasing retail banking or lobby area space to bank employees, officers, directors, principal shareholders, or their immediate families. The letter closed by reminding national banks that any tying arrangements involving the sale of insurance and the granting of credit may violate federal and state antitrust laws.

A more pressing regulatory question, which the letter addressed but which is beyond the boundaries of the OCC's regulatory authority, is whether financial planning, insurance, or securities sales in the bank lobby violates state laws. For example, many state insurance laws bar the payment to or the splitting of commissions with unlicensed parties. As an analogy, the OCC's chief counsel compared the bank's percentage lease situation with that of an independent agent who leases space from a shopping center developer on a percentage basis, writing, in part: "Since, to our knowledge, no state insurance commissioner has taken the position that the agent in this situation is illegally splitting his commissions with unlicensed persons, there should be no cause for questioning a similar arrangement between a bank lessor and an agent."

The Comptroller concluded that, in his opinion, "a national bank may bargain for whatever terms are usual and customary in the leasing of commercial office space. Since the bank must compete with other lessors," he continued, "it ought to be able to compete on the same basis and without restrictions not otherwise required by the need to observe safe and sound banking practice. . . . A lease to an insurance agent based in part on the volume of sales or gross income is a valid lease for a national bank lessor to make."

Are there any regulatory barriers in the securities area? Apparently not. In a footnote to Proposed Rule 3-B-9, issued in October 1983, the SEC stated that it would not disturb net-lease arrangements.

The advantages of a percentage lease can be considerable to the lending institution. First, it is not directly answerable to any regulatory body, except under the relatively straightforward question of referrals. Second, the lessee/lessor relationship between the outside planning firm and the lending institution itself precludes any liability issue from arising against the lessor.

The drawbacks are equally obvious: From a marketing standpoint, the strength of financial planning services lies in the amount of consumer trust they imply and engender. Where marketing materials make it clear that the planning firm and the lending institution are separate and distinct entities, that trust is only obliquely conferred by the bank and only obliquely flows back to it. Once again, the outside planner or turn-key planning firm should be a registered investment advisor pursuant to the Investment Advisers Act.

Investment and Related Products

Insurance Sales

The full implementation of a financial plan will involve the bank or depository institution in the selection of risk management contracts, either directly or by referral to a professional in the field. Although most depository institutions will choose the latter course, the in-house approach may prove more beneficial in the long run. After all, a growing number of the best insurance agents are gaining securities licenses and offering financial planning services on their own.

Lending institutions are expressly prohibited from engaging in the insurance business by the Bank Holding Company Act of 1956 (12 U.S.C. 92 and 12 U.S.C. 24 (Seventh)), with the exception of underwriting and selling "credit life" — that is, insurance contracts which would assure payment of the outstanding balance due on a credit extension if the borrower dies or is disabled. The Federal Reserve Board has since added the somewhat more recent involuntary unemployment contracts to the permitted categories.

With the passage of the Garn-St. Germain Depository Institutions Act of 1982, a number of exceptions were added to this broad prohibition. Among them: the sale of credit life insurance, the extension of property insurance by finance company subsidiaries of bank holding companies where the property was used as collateral, and a little-known provision that allows national banks to conduct any insurance activity "in a place that (i) has a population not exceeding five thousand (as shown by the last preceeding dicennial census), or (ii) the bank holding company, after notice and opportunity for a hearing, demonstrates that its community has inadequate insurance agency facilities" (Title VI(C); 12 U.S.C. 1843(c)(8)).

Basically, that means that if a lending institution is principally domiciled in a town or municipality with less than a 5,000 person population, then it may engage in general insurance agency activities. If not, it will have to establish that presently existing insurance facilities are inadequate, and that insurance services are not available to persons living in the community. Or, as noted earlier, the lending institution could enter into a percentage lease arrangement with a duly licensed insurance agency.

This may be the time to enter into such an arrangement, since a number of states are now looking into the possibility of regulating or restricting percentage lease arrangements. In Connecticut, for example, legislation has been introduced (and later withdrawn) that would have prohibited the leasing insurance agency from using the facilities of the lending institution for mailings, notifications, negotiations of applications or sales literature in any form. The bill also would have prohibited the lending institution from releasing customer lists unless such information would be made available to other insurance agents under similar terms and conditions. The Florida Insurance Department has proposed guidelines that would require fixed rent and contractual limitations on advertising and promotion, while Indiana's state legislature has introduced a bill that would prohibit a lender from using or permitting others to use information in insurance policies of its borrowers in order to solicit sales of insurance or to provide price quotations. The insurance commissioner in Maine has issued definitive guidelines that require any lease between a bank and an insurance agent to provide for a fixed rental payment, and imposes limitations on joint advertising and promotion. The banking commissioner in the same state has proposed a rule that would also require a fixed rent. A bill under consideration in Massachusetts would require fixed rental payments and preclude an agent's use of a bank's mailing list, while Washington's Senate Committee on Financial Institutions has reported out a bill that would prohibit any insurance agent in that state from selling or servicing any insurance policy on the premises of a bank. It would also prohibit any insurance agent under contract with a bank from selling or servicing any insurance policies, whether on or off the premises of a bank.

Recently, the FDIC has raised the possibility that FDIC-insured banks may soon be allowed to underwrite insurance through an internal department. In a proposal dated June 3, 1985, the FDIC reversed an earlier document, and addressed the safety and soundness issues by imposing some restrictions on the bank underwriting activity. Banks would be required to keep insurance departments and their accounting records completely separate from the other banking operations, and the banking company would be prohibited from using its assets to pay for any obligations, liabilities, or expenses of the insurance department. In addition, the insurance department would be restricted from making any investments not permitted for banks.

To protect the consumer in the event of bank failure, departments would be liquidated separately from banks and would not be placed into receivership along with banks.

Variable Annuity Contracts

Variable annuities are a hybrid investment with both annuity and investment characteristics, whereby a customer's premiums are invested in common stocks or other securities, depending on the investment strategy of the company offering the annuities. When it matures, the customer (annuitant) receives payments varying in amount according to a prorated share of the value of the investment portfolio. The variable annuity differs from the traditional fixed annuity in that the return on the former depends entirely on the investment experience of the issuer, whereas the return on the latter is guaranteed.

In a recent opinion letter (Legal Opinion Letter No. 331), the Comptroller's office has determined that Section 16 of the Glass-Steagall Act authorizes banks to buy and sell variable annuities without recourse upon the order and for the account of its customers. The OCC's opinion essentially classified the variable annuity contract as a security, rather than insurance, and noted that the Supreme Court in *Securities Industry Association* vs *Federal Reserve Board* ruled that banks may buy and sell securities for their customers through a discount brokerage subsidiary. In a previous Supreme Court ruling, *Securities and Exchange Commission* vs *United Benefit Life* (387 U.S. at 211), the Court recognized similarities between variable annuities and mutual funds, while the *Investment Company Institute* vs *Camp* (401 U.S. 617; 1971) ruling had determined that variable annuities constitute securities under Section 32 of the Glass-Steagall Act. The proposed activity would not be barred by Section 21 of the Act because the bank would be acting only as an agent, and not buying for its own account. Since the bank would not be underwriting or distributing the variable annuities, the activity would not be prohibited.

The OCC Legal Opinion Letter went on to confront the "safety and soundness" and "salesman's stake" issues directly, suggesting that because the bank would not buy variable annuities contracts for its own account, its assets would not be at risk. This would eliminate the bank's incentive to compromise its duty to render disinterested advice. The bank could provide applications for variable annuities contracts, help customers fill out the applications and forward them to the issuer, receiving a fee on a fixed-commission basis not unlike fees received by discount brokers in the trading of securities. The OCC warned, however, that the bank could not have a quota to sell, and its fee could not vary with the volume of contracts sold.

Mutual Fund Management

Professionally managed pooled equities investments have rapidly become the investment vehicle of choice for the more active IRA/Keogh accounts. Banks that don't offer this alternative will eventually lose retirement account business. Of course, a discount brokerage operation could purchase shares of nationally distributed mutual funds, or the lending institution could recommend that clients deal with a good no-load fund directly. But this will entail a loss of assets, and lose an opportunity to generate fee income while offering a popular personal service.

Several state-chartered nonmember banks and savings and loan associations have sought to rely on Footnote 24 of the *Board of Governors* decision and have established subsidiary corporations to create and operate mutual funds, an activity which was ruled impermissible to banks under the Glass-Steagall Act in *Investment Company Institute* vs *Camp*. The first company to do so was the Boston Five Cents Savings Bank, which organized a subsidiary to distribute its new products back in 1983.

There are four pending cases which revolve around the creation of mutual-fund-like accounts within a bank trust department — an activity which the Comptroller of the Currency has determined to be part of a bank's trust service — a fiduciary service of the bank, rather than a true underwriting activity. The most recent suit has been brought against the Comptroller and Connecticut Bank & Trust by the Investment Company Institute in the U.S. District Court of the District of Connecticut. The other defendants — Citibank, Bank of California, and Wells Fargo — are all selling IRA-type pooled funds.

In all cases, the mutual fund association has taken the legal position that the comingling of IRA assets for investment constitutes the formation of a mutual fund in violation of the Glass-Steagall Act. It has some legal precedent on its side. In September 1984, the District Court for the Northern District of California ruled that the IRA funds of Wells Fargo and the Bank of California "could generate precisely the hazards feared by Congress in enacting Glass-Steagall," and ordered the Comptroller to set aside the approval of such funds. In October, however, the U.S. District Court for the District of Columbia upheld the Comptroller's approval of Citibank's IRA fund. All cases are on appeal, and the general opinion of most observers is that if there are split decisions at the appeals court level, they will eventually reach the Supreme Court, perhaps as early as the summer of 1986.

Limited Partnership Sales

Another popular investment area which is opening up to lending institutions is the real estate limited partnership, particularly those which are tax-advantaged — more commonly known as tax shelters. Why would a depository institution want to enter this complex and often-risky field?

In the area of investment creation/manufacturing, depository institutions will have a natural advantage in the real estate investment market over the majority of syndicators. They know which properties are the best candidates for long-term appreciation, and they know what's going on in their market. In many cases, they have a number of employees whose job is to appraise real estate projects. They often have close ties with local developers. In fact, where a developer comes to the company for a loan which may be too large to handle, syndication would provide an alternative means to raise the capital needed to service the firm's best lending customers, provided, of course, that the underlying economics makes sense for the banking customer.

The syndication market can also be a strong source of fee income. In the most conservatively structured partnerships, roughly 10-15 percent of the offering goes toward management expenses. As much as 8.5 percent of that figure will be a sales commission, a charge the thrift may not want to levy on its regular banking customers. That means that in a small program where, say $3 million is raised, the company could undercut most if not all of the market and still generate $150,000 in fee income plus a potentially lucrative management contract that could be farmed out, and some form of back-end participation upon disposition of the properties.

Finally, and most importantly, creating or offering limited partnership vehicles could be a beneficial service to the bank's upscale clients. By creating and offering one or more income-oriented partnerships with a conservative structure (little or no leverage) the savings and loan association would have a limited-risk investment product that will be competitive with the investment products offered by the more sophisticated brokerage houses and NASD-registered broker-dealers. Coupled with the stocks and bonds, which can be accessed through a discount brokerage service, these limited partnership vehicles would give the company a complete line of investment products for the implementation of a financial plan. This was the philosophy behind a custom-designed real estate partnership offering created by the Robert A. McNeil Corp., one of the larger firms in the syndication business, which was marketed by San Diego-based Great American Savings and Loan.

Already a number of savings and loan associations have entered into this business directly. Some of them, including Butterfield Savings and Loan in Santa Anna, California, and California-based Farmers Savings Bank through Seattle, Washington-based Security Properties, Inc., are manufacturing their own investment products for sales outside of the company as well. Under a recent FDIC proposal, a number of banks may soon be able to engage in similar real estate investment activities directly or through separate subsidiaries. Direct investments, under the proposal, could not exceed 50 percent of the bank's primary capital, and no more than 10 percent could be invested in any one project. If the bank wanted to invest more than 50 percent of its capital, it could do so through one or more separate firms. These investments would not be counted toward a bank's minimum capital requirements, however. The Federal Reserve Board has maintained that state-chartered member banks may not engage in real estate activities, and the Comptroller's office has objected in principle to the FDIC's attempt to impose its legal authority on federally chartered banks.

In the past year, the Office of the Comptroller of the Currency has issued a ruling which would appear to allow lending institutions to sell, on a "best efforts" basis, shares in private placement limited partnerships, those direct participation investments which are sold to "qualified" investors and which are not directly regulated by the SEC. This would allow the banking institution, either directly or through an investment advisory subsidiary or discount brokerage operation, to collect commissions on such investments. Minnesota-based Bankers Systems, Inc., a supplier of turn-key computer-generated financial planning capabilities, is currently offering private placement products through a joint venture subsidiary with Mutual Benefit Life.

The SEC has also been asked to rule on the issue of lending institutions "selling" limited partnership products. In a letter dated March 8, 1984, National Equity Securities Corporation proposed to distribute, on a "best efforts" basis, interests in real estate limited partnerships through federal and state-chartered savings and loan associations. National Equity was itself an NASD-registered broker-dealer subsidiary of Wisconsin-based National Savings, a state-chartered savings and loan association. Its proposal avoided the "arms length" and "safety and soundness" considerations by unequivocally stating that the participating savings and loans would not enter into any commercial loan transactions with the partnerships or their sponsors relating to the acquisition of the partnership properties. Nor would the participating savings and loans handle the investor dollars or the customer securities during the initial purchase.

The sales function, according to the proposal, would be handled by middle management personnel at the participating savings and loan, who would become joint employees of National Equity and the lending institution. They would undergo NASD-licensing procedures to become registered representatives and agents of National Equity, would receive a compliance manual from National Equity, and would be supervised by National Equity in all matters relating to securities activities. The savings and loan association, however, would pay the joint employees' salaries both for their securities and non-securities-related activities. These joint employees would be located at desks on the main floor of the offices of each participating S&L, with conspicuous identification that the joint employee was affiliated with National Equity. Advertisements would refer to the participating S&L only to identify the location where information regarding the partnerships was available, and would clearly disclose the fact that the participating S&L is not a broker-dealer and is separate from National Equity. Even so, the S&L might be called upon to pay all or a portion of the cost of the advertising. The lending institution would be compensated by a percentage of the commissions paid by investors directly to National Equity for all securities transactions initiated on the premises, as compensation for providing office space and equipment and the services of the joint employees.

The SEC's answer to the March 8 letter took the form of a no-action letter from the Chief Counsel's office, dated May 16, 1984, which stated, in part:

> "in view of the fact that National Equity is a registered broker-dealer and all personnel engaged in securities activities will be fully subjected to the regulatory requirements of the federal securities laws and applicable rules of self-regulatory organizations, we would not recommend to the Commission that enforcement action be taken against the S&Ls if S&Ls permit National Equity to distribute the partnerships as described above without the S&Ls registering as broker-dealers under Section 15(b) of the Act."

To date, at least one proposal has been circulated among savings and loan associations as a response to this ruling, which gives an indication of how such arrangements might be structured. It proposes to custom-create limited partnership investments to the depository institution's specifications. These would offer tax-sheltered "dividend-like" returns to the bank (or S&L) customer. The outside company would function as managing general partner, providing all securities and administrative functions (including partnership bookkeeping, real estate acquisition, property management and real estate liquidation) as well as securities licensing and training all of the lending institution's management and marketing personnel.

This kind of structure would appear to offer a number of readily defined advantages. For one thing, it would allow the banking company to enter the syndication business without incurring the significant legal and personnel startup costs that are normally associated with syndication activity. The company could then make a more informed decision about pursuing similar projects in-house after handling one or more investments from a purely sales standpoint.

Having limited partnership shares on the shelf would also allow the structuring of financial services that the company related financial planner could recommend to the more aggressive investor/client. For example, consider an income fund savings account, for direct deposit of quarterly dividends, which could then be reinvested through the discount broker in GNMA collateralized mortgage obligations or municipal bonds, either inside or outside of a bank-administered individual retirement account.

What kind of fees could the lending institution expect to receive for participation in a limited partnership offering? Although the "typical" partnership outlined in the proposal appears to be structured somewhat conservatively compared to the industry standard in the private placement syndication business, it may be a bit aggressive for the taste of some smaller banks or savings and loan associations. For a $20 million offering, the proposal would give $1.4 million back to the participating banking institution — equal to a 7 percent sales commission. All income that would be received from the properties — over and above expenses — would be split 90/10 with the limited partners, with the 10 percent going to the general partners to be split equally between the lending institution and the outside syndicator. Projected return to the participating S&L — assuming (and this is no small assumption) that the investment was meeting projections — would be $533,333.

On the back end, when the properties are sold and the partnership is dissolved, the limited partner investors would receive 85 percent of the sale price. The other 15 percent would be split evenly between the lending institution and the syndicator. The proposal assumes a 48 percent appreciation after six years, which some real estate analysts would find somewhat optimistic. If it holds true, the S&L would stand to make another $339,750, for a total six year return of $2,273,750. The syndicator, of course, receives a like amount, plus up to $200,000 in underwriting fees, 5 percent or 6 percent of the gross revenues as a property management fee and a 3 percent real estate commission on the back-end sale to a real estate subsidiary.

Even if the lending institution chooses not to collect commissions on the sale of direct participation securities, it could still add them to its menu of investment products, and collect some sort of a flat fee for performing an investment research service. Under these conditions, it is important for the bank to have the capabilities, either inside or outside, to thoroughly evaluate the investments that are currently on the market.

Since limited partnership investments are typically extremely complicated both structurally and from a day-to-day managerial standpoint, it is generally advisable to contract with outside due diligence experts whose business is to evaluate partnerships. Rhode Island Hospital Trust, for example, contracts with Roe, Martin and Neiman, a law firm in Atlanta, for such services. In Denver, a company called Planned Management Company offers the same services to a number of banks and savings and loan associations.

Conclusion

What can we conclude from this? At this writing, the House and Senate are debating the merits of a banking bill which would either significantly expand the powers enjoyed by depository institutions, or halt the gradual erosion of regulatory barriers. It is the third major bill in the past four years.

In the area of financial planning, however, the regulatory barriers appear to be already breached beyond repair. Lending institutions, particularly those that are not members of the Federal Reserve system, have legal and regulatory precedent to enter the full service retail securities business, and to provide counsel and guidance to clients concerning every small detail of their financial lives.

For the reader, this knowledge confers an unusual degree of power. Most of your competitors in the banking industry are uncertain about the services they can legally offer. Many will continue to watch Congressional actions, hoping to see a specific blessing on financial planning services signed into law. Without that blessing, navigating through the various regulatory channels will not be easy. But the company that succeeds in establishing the service under these guidelines could enjoy as much as a two-year lead on the rival banks and savings and loan associations in its market, and could capture market share from the vendors in other sectors of the financial services industry as well. This could prove to be a distinct advantage.

6

Securities Law

There is a great controversy involved here, and it seems to me that there comes a point at which you can manage a certain number of issues in terms of resolving them, and beyond that you may not be able to do so.

Senator Donald Riegle
Describing the debate over the Garn-St Germain Depository Institutions Act, 9/24/82

The Complexity of Compliance

If a lending institution decides to create a subsidiary which offers financial planning services, it will have to meet the requirements of a new regulatory structure which governs securities firms. If the new company plans to provide securities investment advice to others for compensation, it will be required to register with the Securities and Exchange Commission (SEC) and comply with the SEC's interpretive rulings of the Investment Advisers Act of 1940. If its executives plan to sell securities products or otherwise implement its financial plans, they will have to register the company as a broker-dealer with the National Association of Securities Dealers (NASD), a self-regulatory organization that reports to the SEC, under the Securities Exchange Act of 1934.

If, on the other hand, the lending institution enters into a joint venture relationship with an outside vendor, financial planner, or broker-dealer, the registration, record keeping requirements, and other regulatory chores would fall primarily on the outside firm. Even in this case, however, the joint venturing lending institution should be aware of what these chores entail. They should periodically review procedures to ensure that they are in full compliance.

The Legal Foundation of Securities Regulations

To understand the often-complex securities regulations and requirements, it is necessary to look at their legal foundations. The world of securities and risk management has a long history of federal and state regulation, much of it dating back to the same post-Depression era when the present banking laws began to take shape. Today, planners and their activities fall under the purview of the Securities Act of 1933 (15 U.S.C. paragraphs 77a-77aa), the Securities Exchange Act of 1934 (15 U.S.C. paragraphs 78a-78jj), the Employment Retirement Income Security Act (Pub. L. No. 93-406, 88 Stat. 829) and, most importantly, the Investment Advisers Act of 1940 (15 U.S.C. paragraphs 80b-1-80b-21).

These are administered, clarified, and amplified by a large and growing body of federal officials. At last count, there were at least 10 federal regulatory agencies who exercise some degree of authority

over financial planning professionals, with the tightest control re-
served for those who offer the more comprehensive services on the
market, including specific investment and risk management advice.
This is in addition to the various state securities and insurance ad-
ministrators, whose authority can be considerably more direct and
immediate than Washington's, plus such standard-setting organizations as the International Association for Financial Planning (IAFP)
and its Registry program. Beyond that lies a considerable body of
inter-professional regulation that securities representatives, insurance agents, accountants, and lawyers have to meet.

The SEC — Chief Among Regulators

Chief among the regulators, of course, is the Securities and Exchange Commission, which was granted broad authority to admin-
ister the Investment Advisers Act by Congress in 1960. The provision
directly authorizes the SEC to adopt rules and regulations as it finds
necessary and, further, seeks to:

1. provide additional grounds for denying, suspending or revok-
   ing the registration of an investment advisor

2. grant new power to postpone, within certain limits, the effectiveness of an application for registration

3. empower the Commission by rule and regulation to require
   the keeping of such books and records and the filing of such
   reports by investment advisors as it may prescribe, and permit the periodic examination of such books and records by
   the Commission

4. empower the Commission by rule and regulation to define
   and prescribe means reasonably designed to prevent fraudulent, deceptive, or manipulative practices.

Components of an Investment Advisor

As we saw in the previous chapter, the SEC's definition of an
investment advisor has three components. First, the advisor must
give advice about securities. What is a security? Section 202(a)(18)
offers a somewhat lengthy definition which includes, among other

things, stocks, bonds, debentures, notes or other evidences of indebt-edness, certificates of interest or participation in profit-sharing agreements, investment contracts, fractional undivided interests in oil, gas, or other mineral rights, puts, calls, straddles, and options.

Under the second test, the advisor must be in the business of advising others. Third, the advisor must be receiving some form of compensation for his or her services. These would appear to be straightforward tests, but in a release dated August 13, 1981, the SEC spelled out exactly what the Commissioners look for when deciding who should register under the 1940 Act:

> *Whether or not a person's activities constitute being en-gaged in the business of advising others as to the value of securities or the advisability of investing in securities or issuing reports or analyses concerning securities as part of a regular business will depend on 1) whether the investment advice being provided is solely incidental to a non-investment-advisory primary business of the per-son providing the advice; 2) the specificity of the advice being given; and 3) whether the provider of the advice is receiving, directly or indirectly, any special compensa-tion therefore. (Securities Release No. IA-770)*

Does every financial planner fall under the definitions outlined in this language? Probably not. It appears that non-specific advice, as interpreted by the SEC involves even the simple discussion in gen-eral terms of the advisability of investing in securities in the context of the client's overall financial plan. Although it is not clear what the SEC release means when it refers to specific categories of securities, but advice to invest in the stock market, equity and debt securities, or tax-advantaged limited partnerships would probably be regarded as general enough not to make the financial planner, by definition, an investment advisor. If he offers advice any more specific than that, however, registration would be required.

To avoid "special compensation," the planner would have to forego any definable charge for securities advice, charging only an overall or hourly fee for financial planning services. If the financial planner received any separatable fees for the investment advisory portion of his or her total services, or received any direct or indirect compensation in connection with a client's purchase or sale of securities, then the planner would be deemed to be in the investment advisory business and registration would be required.

Section 203 lists three additional exemptions, which probably will not cover the bank-affiliated financial planning department. The first is specified for advisors who have clients who are residents of the state in which the advisor practices, provided that the company does not furnish advice regarding listed securities or enjoys unlisted trading privileges on any national securities exchange. The second is provided to advisors whose only clients are insurance companies. The third includes all advisors who, during the preceeding twelve months, had fewer than fifteen clients, who do not hold themselves out to the public as investment advisors, and who do not advise certain enumerated categories of companies.

Failure to register when it is appropriate to do so can have serious consequences. Both the Investment Advisers Act and the Securities Exchange Act explicitly provide for voiding contracts when performance involves a violation of the statute. Thus, clients of an investment advisor who is operating in violation of the registration requirements have the right to rescind their transactions or obtain damages. Willful failure to register also carries specific criminal penalties, including fines of up to $10,000 and imprisonment for up to five years. The SEC also has the power to deny an application for registration if there has been a past willful violation of federal securities laws.

Registration as Investment Advisor

Section 203 of the Investment Advisers Act also specifies the registration provisions for those who meet the tests as an investment advisor, and do not fall into one of the exemption categories. This includes filing Form ADV with the Securities and Exchange Commission, along with a one-time $150 registration fee. On April 5, 1985, the North American Securities Administrators Association (NASAA) adopted a revised Form ADV, which was formally incorporated into the SEC's application process on January 1, 1986, in order to eliminate duplication of effort on the state and federal level.

Basically, Form ADV is a questionnaire that calls for information regarding the advisor's name, form and place of organization, nature of business activities, scope of authority with respect to clients' funds and accounts, basis of compensation, and background information designed to uncover any illegalities the applicant may have been charged with or convicted of in the past.

Any applicant who proposes to take custody or possession of client funds or securities, or requires prepayment of advisory fees six months or more in advance and in excess of $500 has some additional burdens: filing a balance sheet audited by an independent public account and prepared in accordance with generally accepted accounting principles. Among the items included in the new form that were not a part of the old is one to identify advisors engaged in financial planning services. This section asks how the applicant charges for investment advisory services (percentage of assets under management, hourly charges, fixed fees, commissions, etc.), who the planning clients are likely to be (individuals, banks, investment companies, or pension and profit sharing plans), types of securities the applicant will give advice about, and appears to call for a number of essays concerning the planning firm's methods of analysis, sources of information, and investment strategies.

Once the registration documents are filed, the application will become effective 45 days later, unless the SEC institutes proceedings to deny prior to that time. Registrants are required to keep their registration current by filing amendments and a short annual report on Form ADV-S. In addition, under Rule 204-3 (the "brochure rule"), registrants are required to provide clients and prospective clients with pertinent information about the advisor, its business background and practices, and to deliver or offer in writing to existing clients similar information on an annual basis without charge. Under virtually all circumstances, this is the information contained in Part II of Form ADV.

Recordkeeping Requirements

Probably the most complex and often-referred to group of regulations under the Investment Advisers Act have to do with the recordkeeping requirements. These are contained in Section 204, entitled "Annual and Other Reports," a deceptively short 144-word section which essentially transfers broad authority to the SEC to make rules in this area, requiring, in part, that advisors "make and keep for prescribed periods such records . . . as the Commission . . .

may prescribe as necessary or appropriate in the public interest or for the protection of investors." It also allows the Commission to make periodic examinations of the records maintained by registered investment advisors.

To implement these general items of concern, the SEC has promulgated Rule 204-1 and Rule 204-2, which specify precisely what is required of investment advisors. These can be generally divided into the usual accounting books and related documents that should be kept in any well-run business, and those records that reflect the fiduciary nature of the advisory business. In addition to identifying the books and records that must be maintained, the Rule also establishes the retention periods for records after the fiscal year in which the last entry was made and allows microfilm or microfiche to be substituted for paper copies after two years. Finally, the Rule provides non-resident advisors with two options on supplying the Commission with copies of their books and records.

Rule 204-1 and the first six subparagraphs of Rule 204-2(a) concern the basic financial records which the investment advisor should maintain. These include Form ADV and up-to-date amendments, ADV-S and all journals, general and auxiliary ledgers, checkbooks, bank statements, bills or statements of account, trial balance and financial statements. The Rule does not define what the format of these records should be, and it appears that each advisor is free to design and use those accounting books and records which best meet the specific requirements of his or her business, so long as they use generally accepted principles. In fact, in Item (a)(2), there is a specific provision that allows other records to be used in place of traditional ledger accounts, which means that a series of other records, if they contain the information usually found in a ledger, can be used in place of a separate ledger record. The Rule is also silent on the question of whether an advisor's accounting records should be maintained on the cash, modified accrual, or accrual basis.

Item (a)(3) requires the preparation of a memorandum for each order given by the advisor for the purchase or sale of any security, and of any instruction received by the advisor from a client concerning the purchase, sale, receipt, or delivery of a security. Where these are received orally, as is most often the case, the advisor is required to make a written record. The precise format is not specified, but the record must include the terms and conditions of the order, an identification of the person connected with the advisor who made the recommendation and the name of the client, the date of entry and the bank, and the broker or dealer by or through whom the order was executed. In general, this memorandum can be attached to the confirmation of order execution, creating a complete record of each transaction in one place.

The records which the SEC requires as a result of the special fiduciary nature of the advisor's business make up a somewhat longer category. Items (a)(7) and (a)(11) concern written materials produced and distributed by the advisor or received by the advisor. Market letters, reports and advertisements which contain a recommendation of a specific security and which are sent by the advisor to ten or more persons, must either contain the basis for the advisor's recommendations in the communication itself or be filed with an attached memorandum which states the basis of the recommendation. (Clients receiving investment supervisory services, defined as giving continuous advice about the investment of funds on the basis of each client's individual need, are exempted from being counted in this "rule of 10.")

All other written materials sent or received by an investment advisor are to be maintained according to Item (a)(7), which sets forth three classifications of written materials: 1) recommendations or advice given or proposed to be given; 2) the receipt, disbursement, or delivery of client funds and securities; and 3) the placing or execution of any order to purchase or sell any security of any client. The recommendations and advice category is not limited to securities. Any advice of any kind, if in writing, appears to be subject to review and should be kept in the advisor's files. Letters received from clients inquiring about the services or advice being provided or offering complaints also would fall into this category. If the recommendations or advice are given orally, however, no written record must be prepared.

It appears that advertisements, insofar as they relate to attempting to obtain clients to whom the advisor will give (sell) advice, fall under this category as well, although no provision specifically sets this forth. The Rule does not expressly require that all working papers and other supporting documents used in developing the content of any advertisement be maintained. The SEC's staff, however, during an inspection reserves the right to ask the advisor to justify the performance data being used in advertisements, in order to determine if the data is misleading. By implication, Item (a)(7) requires that the names and addresses of persons receiving advertisements by mail be maintained where the number does not exceed 10. If 10 or more are sent an advertisement, their names and addresses would not have to be maintained. If the mailing is sent to members of a list, however, a memorandum describing the list and its source should be maintained.

What about materials that are received by the advisor? The SEC has taken the position that those that relate to recommendations or advice given or proposed to be given should be maintained. The advisor should keep files for all research reports and other materials received if they are used in the process of providing advice. The company is under no obligation to save unsolicited market letters or materials of general public distribution, however, nor is it required to keep periodicals of regular public distribution such as newspapers and magazines.

Items (a)(8) and (a)(9) relate to advisors who have powers of attorney or discretionary powers over client assets, a situation which will probably not apply to an SEC-regulated lending institution-affiliated entity. In general, they require that the advisor keep and maintain a list of discretionary accounts and written evidence of the advisor's authority. Rule 204(2)(b)(1) specifies a number of additional recordkeeping responsibilities that are required under these circumstances. The advisor must maintain a journal or other record showing all purchases, sales, receipts, and deliveries of securities, including certificate numbers for such accounts and all other debits and credits to these accounts, cash receipts to and payments from funds of these clients, as well as the receipt and delivery of such other assets as real estate and commodities. In addition, Rule 206(4)-2-a(5) requires that all funds and securities in the custody or possession of an advisor be verified by actual examination at least once each calendar year. The advisor must also maintain copies of confirmations received for all transactions effected by or for the account of any custody client. Finally, Item (b)(4) requires the advisor to establish and maintain on a current basis a separate record for each security in which any such client has a position, essentially a ledger account by security for each security in which any custody client has a position.

Item (a)(10) requires that any written agreement (including such ubiquitous contracts as rental and service agreements, mortgages, employment contracts, and contracts with clients for investment advisory services) be maintained in some orderly manner. Although it is not specifically required that investment advisory contracts be in written form, there are some good reasons for maintaining them that way. Section 205(2) of the Investment Advisers Act requires that the contract provide in substance that it cannot be assigned without the client's consent. With an oral contract, this may be difficult if not impossible to establish.

The remaining three subparagraphs of Rule 204-2(a) involve recordkeeping requirements concerning personal securities transactions, disclosure documents, and client solicitation agreements. Item (a)(12) and (a)(13) require that the advisor maintain a record of every securities transaction in which the advisor acquires any direct or indirect interest in the security. This is designed to allow SEC examiners to determine if an advisor is violating his or her fiduciary relationship through personal securities trading activities (e.g., purchasing securities for his or her own account before recommending them to clients, then selling his or her own holdings once the price has risen). The record must include the title and amount of the security involved, the date and nature of transaction, the price at which it was effected and the name of the broker, dealer, or bank through whom the transaction was effected.

Item (a)(14) sets forth the SEC's interpretation of the "brochure rule," defining the written statements or disclosure documents which advisors are required to give their clients under Rule 204-3 of the Investment Advisers Act. In general, it states that all advisors must provide clients with a written disclosure statement at the beginning of the advisor/client relationship and on an annual basis thereafter, which describes the advisor's activities, fees, relationships, security evaluation methods, and other important information that is contained in Part II of Form ADV. For its own records, the advisor must keep a copy of each written statement and every amendment or revision given or sent to any client, along with the dates that they were given or offered to be given to all clients and persons who subsequently bcome clients.

How long must the books and records required under Rule 204-2 be retained? Paragraph (e) specifies that they must be retained for at least five years from the end of the fiscal year in which the last entry in the records was made, and that during the first two of those years, they should be stored in the advisor's offices. Further, during the first two years, they must be stored in hard copy format. After that, the books and records may be microfilmed or microfiched. For the remaining three years, they should be preserved in an easily accessible place, such as a records storage building away from the advisor's offices. For partnership articles and amendments, articles of incorporation, charters, minute books, and stock certificate books of the advisor, however, the SEC requires that the advisor or its principals maintain complete records until at least three years after termination of the enterprise.

State Regulations

In addition to federal registration, the would-be investment advisory firm may be required to establish and maintain registration with the local state securities commissioner. Currently, 38 states, along with the jurisdictions of Puerto Rico and Guam, require advisors to register. If the lending institution resides in Alabama, Arizona, Colorado, Georgia, Iowa, Maine, Maryland, Massachusetts, North Carolina, Ohio, Vermont, or Wyoming, there is no state application process, although the Maryland legislature is due to vote on a regulatory bill. Hawaii and Virginia do not require registration if the advisory firm is already registered with the SEC.

Although some jurisdictions permit advisors to file Form ADV in lieu of a separate state form, many require the filing of supplementary forms and schedules containing additional information. Their definitions of an investment advisor generally follow the lead of the Investment Advisers Act, although there may be some variations in the wording. Michigan's Uniform Securities Act provides a definition whose language is more or less typical. Under Section 451.601 of the State Act, an investment advisor is defined as:

> *Any person who, for consideration, engages in the business of advising others, either directly or through publications or writings, as to the value of securities or commodity contracts, or as to the advisability of investing in, purchasing or selling securities or commodity con-*

tracts who, for consideration as part of a regular business, issues or promulgates analyses or reports concerning securities or commodity contracts, or who acts as a finder in conjunction with the offer, sale, or purchase of a security or commodity. "Investment advisor" does not include:

(1) a bank, savings institution or trust company,

(2) a lawyer, accountant, engineer, geologist, geophysicist or teacher whose performance of these services is solely incidental to the practice of his or her profession;

(3) a broker-dealer or registered agent acting on behalf of a broker-dealer whose performance of these services is solely incidental to the conduct of his or her business as a broker-dealer;

(4) a publisher of any bona fide newspaper, news magazine or business or financial publication of general, regular and paid circulation;

(5) a person who has no place of business in this state if (A) his only clients in this state are other investment advisors, broker-dealers, banks, savings institutions, trust companies, insurance companies, investment companies as defined in the Investment Company Act of 1940, pension or profit-sharing trusts the assets of which are managed by a bank or trust company or other institutional manager, or other financial institution or institutional buyers, whether acting for themselves or as trustees, or (B) during any period of 12 consecutive months he does not direct business communications into this state in any manner to more than five clients other than those specified in clause (A), whether or not he or any of the persons to whom the communications are directed is then present in this state;

(6) such other persons not within the intent of this paragraph as the administrator may, by rule or order, designate; or

(7) a trustee whose custody of assets is pursuant to judicial appointment, or appointment under a trust

*indenture, or agreement and who does not hold himself
out to the general public as giving advice to others with
respect to securities, and who maintains close contact
with the personal financial affairs of his client as a part
of his fiduciary responsibilities, or a person who gives
advice only to such a trustee.*

In addition to registration, a number of states impose added restrictions or regulatory hurdles which should be investigated locally prior to the startup of the planning service. For example, the Connecticut Uniform Security Act requires written consent from the state securities commissioner in order for a person to be concurrently registered as an agent of more than one investment advisor — a situation that could arise under some joint venture structures that were discussed in the previous chapter. The Pennsylvania Securities Act of 1972 goes so far as to require substantial prior investment advisory experience of all applications. Under Section 303, no individual will be registered unless he or she:

*has been engaged in business as a principal of a broker-
dealer or investment advisor or as an employee of a broker-dealer or investment advisor in other than a clerical
capacity, or has occupied some other position satisfac-
tory to the Commission in the securities, banking, finance or other related business on a substantially full-
time basis during the two year period immediately prior
to the filing of the application or during three of the five
years immediately preceding such filing.*

Passage of some forms of competency examination is required of investment advisors practicing in Alaska, California, Delaware, Florida, Kansas, Missouri, Montana, Nebraska, New Jersey, New Mexico, North Dakota, Oklahoma, Oregon, Pennsylvania, Rhode Island, Texas, Utah, Washington, West Virginia, and Wisconsin. In some cases, this requirement may be met through federal registration processes. Both the North Dakota Securities Act of 1951 and the Alaska Securities Act of 1959 provide an exemption from examination requirements for all applicants who have passed the NASD registration requirements.

Similarly, registration fees will vary widely, from $15 in Kansas to $300 in Arkansas and Oklahoma and $400 in New Hampshire. Some states require the investment advisory applicant to file a surety bond. In Mississippi, Missouri, Delaware, Kansas, and Oregon, the bond amount is $10,000 for all applicants with less than $25,000 in assets. Kentucky, New Hampshire, Virginia, and Minnesota require a surety bond of up to $25,000. In Michigan, it may reach as high as $100,000. In Florida, state officials prefer a different approach: they take a complete set of fingerprints from each applicant or the principal of corporate applicants, which are sent to the Federal Bureau of Investigation.

Once the application has been accepted, other state laws may govern the planner/client relationship. The investment contract is a subject of popular concern. In Arkansas, Subsection 67-1236(b) of the state Uniform Securities Act provides that all investment advisory contracts specify, in writing:

> *(1) that the investment advisor shall not be compensated on the basis of a share of capital gains upon or capital appreciation of the funds or any portion of the funds of the client;*
>
> *(2) that no assignment of the contract may be made by the investment advisor without the consent of the other party to the contract; and*
>
> *(3) that the investment advisor, if a partnership, shall notify the other party to the contract of any change in the membership of the partnership within a reasonable time after the change.*

California's Corporate Securities Law of 1968 prohibits investment advisory contracts which

> *(1) provides for compensation to the investment advisor on the basis of a share of capital gains upon or capital appreciation of the funds of any portion of the funds of the client, except as may be permitted by rule of the commissioner;*
>
> *(2) fails to provide, in substance, that no assignment of such contract shall be made by the investment advisor without the consent of the other party to the contract; or*

(3) fails to provide, in substance, that the investment advisor, if a partnership, will notify the other party to the contract of any changes in the membership of such partnership within a reasonable time after such change.

There may also be restrictions on the kind of advertisement, circular, letter, or other written communications that may be distributed to more than one client or potential client. Typically, these provisions specifically concern any report or analysis of specific investment opportunities, but they may be broad enough to include even the most general investment advisory service with respect to securities. Since one of the chief services of financial planners is the production of a financial plan, and since boilerplate text could bring this document under the broad definition of an advertisement, this can be an important area to check in the startup phases of operation. For example, in Connecticut an investment advisor is prohibited from distributing any advertisement:

(aaa) which refers, directly or indirectly, to any testimonial of any kind concerning the investment advisor or concerning any advice, analysis, report or other service rendered by such investment advisor; or

(bbb) which refers, directly or indirectly, to past specific recommendations of such investment advisor which were or would have been profitable to any person; provided, however, that this shall not prohibit an advertisement which sets out or offers to furnish a list of all recommendations made by such investment advisor within the immediately preceding period of not less than one year of such advertisement, and such list if it is furnished separately:

(1) state the name of each such security recommended, the date and nature of each such recommendation (e.g., whether to buy, sell or hold), the market price at that time, the price at which the recommendation was to be acted upon, and the market price of each such security as of the most recent practicable date, and

(2) contain the following cautionary legend on the first page thereof in print or type used in the body or text

thereof: "it should not be assumed that recommendations made in the future will be profitable or will equal the performance of the securities in this list"; or

(ccc) which represents, directly or indirectly, that any graph, chart, formula or other device being offered can in and of itself be used to determine which securities to buy and sell, or when to buy or sell them; or which represents, directly or indirectly, that any graph, chart, formula or other device being offered will assist any person in making his or her own decisions as to which securities to buy or sell, or when to buy or sell them, without prominently disclosing in such advertisement the limitations thereof, and the difficulties with respect to its use; or

(ddd) which contains any statement to the effect that any report, analysis or other service will be furnished free or without charge, unless such report, analysis or other service actually is or will be furnished entirely free and without any condition or obligation, directly or indirectly; or

(eee) which contains any untrue statement of a material fact, or which is otherwise false or misleading.

An analogous provision in the Oregon Securities Law reads a bit differently, but contains the same basic provisions.

Broker-Dealer Registration

When a depository institution offers discount brokerage services, it should be registered to stock and sell securities. If, on the other hand, the company establishes a subsidiary or joint venture entity which will place investment products into client portfolios, it will also be necessary to register as a broker-dealer. In many cases, this will be a separate entity from that which offers the advisory services, a structure which helps avoid any confusion in the customer's mind between advisory and sales activities.

The filing requirements for would-be broker-dealers are described in the Securities Exchange Act of 1934. The term "broker" is defined there as "any person engaged in the business of effecting transactions in securities for the account of others." (Banks are specifically excluded.) The term "dealer" is defined as any person "engaged in the business of buying and selling securities for his or her own account, either individually or in some fiduciary capacity, but not as a part of a regular business." As in the case of the investment advisor, the "engagement in the business" definition requires a more than incidental participation in the regulated activity, rather than the actual practice of it as a full-time occupation. Of course, the presence of investment-related compensation would cause the planner to fit the statutory definitions of a broker-dealer. A financial planner who simply brings together the buyer and seller, who then go on to deal directly with each other, would probably not come under these definitions.

Broker-dealer applications with the SEC and NASAA's state securities commissioner are addressed to the Central Registration Depository, which transmits the information electronically to the Commission and all jurisdictions in which the advisor was registering for review and granting of registration.

The SEC's broker-dealer application is Form BD, which carries no filing fee. Form BD basically asks for little more than the basic information about the company, including name, location, and any affiliations. Applicants must also present a statement of financial condition, showing the nature and amount of assets, liabilities and net worth of the applicant, a computation of the applicant's aggregate indebtedness and net capital; disclosures about the capital, financing, and facilities required to carry on the proposed broker-dealer business; and an oath or affirmation of the accuracy of the information.

As with investment advisors, once an application has been accepted by the SEC for filing, it will grant the registration or institute proceedings to determine whether registration should be denied within 45 days. Thereafter, the broker-dealer must maintain adequate books and records, and file quarterly and annual reports with the SEC, containing audited financial statements. The company must also comply with the SEC's securities transaction-confirmation requirements and meet minimum net-capital requirements: Those who do not hold funds or securities for, or owe money or securities to clients generally are permitted to maintain minimum net capital of either $5,000 or $2,500. For those that do undertake to trade on behalf of clients, the minimum net capital requirement is $25,000.

Under the Securities Exchange Act, all registered broker-dealers must become members of the NASD. Members must qualify at two levels: one for principals, the other for registered representatives who perform the actual sales functions. The NASD has established five different categories for principal registration: general securities, financial and operations, investment company products and variable contracts, direct participation programs, and options. Registered representatives can register to sell in three different categories: 1) general securities products; 2) investment company products; or 3) variable contracts or direct participation programs. Each requires a competency examination; applications must be accompanied by a $500 fee, plus $40 for each exam to be taken. An additional measure of regulatory authority is the Securities Investor Protection Corporation (SIPC), in which all registered broker-dealers automatically become members. The SIPC is administered by its own board, and has jurisdiction over broker-dealers in the event of insolvency.

Liability Issues

Unlike those in the investment advisory market, the liabilities that can arise from broker-dealer activities are relatively straightforward. As in the case of the Advisers Act, contracts made in violation of or involving performance in violation of any provision of the Exchange Act generally are deemed to be void in a court of law. Clients cannot sue for a failure to register as a broker-dealer. Violating the Exchange Act's antifraud provisions (including misstatements or misleading omissions of material facts or the use of manipulative, deceptive or fraudulent acts in connection with securities transactions) would, however, offer the client an implied right of action.

In general, broker-dealers are subject to something called the "shingle theory," which basically means that simply by going into the securities business, they by implication are testifying that they will deal fairly with their customers. Broker-dealers are precluded from charging prices that are not reasonably related to the market price in principal transactions, making a recommendation without reasonable basis, or excessively trading customers' accounts to generate commission dollars. They are also prohibited from recommending the purchase of securities not suitable for a particular customer, although there is no fiduciary duty implied in the client relationship.

The financial planning service, on the other hand, implies a fiduciary duty to clients, which places a much greater degree of legal responsibility on the service provider. Wherever specific investment advice will be offered to clients, liability issues are raised which may not be immediately obvious, but which should confronted in the initial stages of the planning program. Whether the advisory services are offered in-house or through a relationship with an external planning firm, the investment advisor should limit liability exposure by maintaining professional liability insurance for any errors and omissions which may be alleged in the course of its practice. Ideally, this would specifically cover financial planning services, and would thus assist the bank in securing the benefits of the financial planning services while avoiding some of the risks involved in the business.

At present, such a policy is only available through a negotiated agreement by the IAFP. Its terms include activities involved in tax shelters, energy investments, commodity investments, life insurance sales, property and casualty insurance sales, real estate investments, the rendering of financial planning advice and the design of financial plans. Excluded is legal advice by attorneys, dishonest, deliberate or fraudulent acts, willful violation of the Securities Act of 1933 and the Securities Exchange Act of 1934, or guarantees of investment performance. The policy itself should be examined to determine the breadth of the exclusion for any contractual liability, such as in a contract with a bank, and for costs of defense coverage.

The regulatory prohibitions and potential legal liabilities that are part of the financial planning service are somewhat complex, in part because it is too new to have accumulated the body of case law and regulatory attention that can be found associated with more longstanding professions. Under Section 205-5 of the Investment Advisers Act, investment advisors are prohibited from entering into contracts, provide fees on the basis of a share of the capital appreciation of the client's portfolio, or fail to provide that no assignment of such contract can be made by the advisor without the consent of the other party of the contract. Section 203(e) enumerates a rather longer list of prohibitions: the investment advisor's registration may be revoked or limited if a company principal has made false statements in the initial application or subsequent reports to the SEC, if he or she has been convicted within the past ten years of any felony or misdemeanor connected with securities fraud, bribery, perjury, burglary, forgery, or other specified crime, if he or she is temporarily enjoined by a court of law, has willfully violated federal securities law or failed to sufficiently supervise an employee who subsequently committed a violation of federal securities law.

The Investment Advisers Act also contains antifraud provisions which make it unlawful for an investment advisor to "employ any device, scheme or artifice to defraud any client or prospective client," or to "engage in any transaction, practice or course of business which operates as a fraud or deceit upon any client or prospective client." The SEC's interpretive release No. IA-770 reiterates this point. Legally, the standards that govern a fiduciary relationship are much more stringent than those that govern sales activities, in part because it can be assumed that the client reposes trust and confidence in the financial planner to take all necessary actions to improve his or her personal financial situation.

As a fiduciary, an investment advisor has a duty of loyalty to clients, and must act solely in the clients' interests. In the 1963 case *SEC vs Capital Gains Research Bureau, Inc.*, the Supreme Court held that an investment advisor is a fiduciary which owes its clients "an affirmative duty of utmost good faith, and full fair disclosure of all material facts." Although the Supreme Court ruled that a client may not sue for breach of the antifraud provisions of the Advisers Act, there is nothing to prevent a client from bringing an action for damages based on breach of fiduciary duty, which is grounded in state law, or based on state-law definitions of fraud. Of equal importance, any advisory contract which involves performance that is found to be in violation of any provision of the Investment Advisers Act is deemed void. This would allow the injured client to assert a private claim for rescission of the investment advisory agreement and for restitution of any fees paid thereunder.

Exercising Reasonable Care

The most crucial element of the financial planner's investment advisory functions is the responsibility to analyze client data and prepare a financial plan. In this process, from a legal standpoint, the planner needs to exercise reasonable care, which basically means that he or she should do what other reasonably competent planners would do under the same or similar circumstances. In cases like this, negligence will be determined based on the extent to which the planner's conduct deviated from the accepted norms within the profession. Thus, standards of care are established by the profession itself. These include, in addition to matters testified by expert witnesses based on experience in the field, such written documentation as the IAFP's Code of Professional Ethics, which is subscribed to by some 25,000 people in the marketplace. The Code charges members to:

1. Endeavor as professionals to place the public interest above their own

2. Seek continually to maintain and improve their professional knowledge, skills, and competence

3. Obey all laws and regulations and avoid any contact or activity which would cause unjust harm to others

4. Be diligent in the performance of their occupational duties

5. Establish and maintain honorable relationships with other professionals, with those whom the members serve in a professional capacity, and with all those who rely upon members' professional judgments and skills

6. Assist in improving the public's understanding of financial planning

7. Use the fact of membership in a manner consistent with the Code

8. Assist in maintaining the integrity of the Code.

To fall under the definition of reasonable care, the planner must also make use of standard techniques and tools when forming a diagnosis of the client's financial position, and in making ultimate recommendations. Even if the recommendations differ from those of his or her colleagues, the client would not be able to bring suit on that basis alone. When recommending a specific security, the planner must also disclose all relevant information about the proposed investment to the client, including the investment's objectives, risks, and potential benefits. If these facts are withheld, the planner could be held liable in an action alleging negligence as well as common law fraud or deceit.

The planner has an obligation to keep current on all relevant changes in the tax law as well as specific investment strategies, current knowledge and practice in the field.

Conclusion

By way of conclusion, it should be noted that the securities regulatory bodies are rapidly assimilating a wide variety of new applicants, and have demonstrated a willingness to deal fairly with nontraditional service providers. At this writing, the NASD is entering its third consecutive year of record numbers of applications, while the SEC is exploring the possibility of regulating the sudden upsurge in investment advisors through a self-regulatory organization formed by the IAFP.

For most lending institutions, one of the biggest obstacles to overcome in the formation of financial planning capabilities is fear of the unknown. In this case, that unknown involves concern over entering a new regulatory structure. While this book is not designed as a comprehensive guide to all the responsibilities that come with SEC and NASD registration, familiarity with this chapter should help the reader understand the broad general areas of concern, and avoid the worst of the inevitable headaches that accompany any new venture.

Appendixes

Appendix I   Personal Financial Planning Software

Appendix II   Discount Brokers Offering Services To Banks

Appendix III   Correspondent Banks Offering Discount Brokerage Services To Other Banks

Appendix IV   Market Research Firms

Appendix V   Colleges and Universities Affiliated With The Certified Financial Planner (CFP) Program

Appendix VI   Case Studies

I

Personal Financial Planning Software

Exexplan II. Sawhney Software, 888 Seventh Avenue, New York, NY 10106, 212-541-8020, $6,000. Major features: income tax planning, income & cash flow, net worth, investment analysis, portfolio detail. Requires IBM XT/AT or compatible; 512 RAM; 5 megabyte hard disk drive.

Fastplan. Abacus Data Systems, Inc., 722 Genevieve Street, Suite C, Solana Beach, CA 92075, 619-755-0505, $3495. Major features: income tax planning, income & cash flow, net worth, investment analysis, portfolio detail. Includes a fully integrated data base manager [dBase II RunTime] and mailing features.

Financial & Estate Planner's NumberCruncher-I. Stephan R. Leimberg & Robert T. LeClair, Financial Data Corp., Box 1332, Bryn Mawr, PA 19010, 215-896-4525, $110+. Major features: income tax planning, income & cash flow, net worth, investment analysis. Template system for Lotus 1-2-3 computer worksheet.

Financial Planning System. Bankers Systems Financial Services, Inc., P.O. Box 97, St. Cloud, MN, 612-251-3060, $9,500. Major features: income tax planning, income & cash flow, net worth, investment analysis. Not a micro system. Works on IBM system 34 or 36, or service bureau is available to which you mail in input.

Financial Profiles. Financial Profiles, Inc., 23201 Mill Creek Road, Laguna Hills, CA 92653, 714-859-8400, 800-437-7687, $895+. Major features: income tax planning, income & cash flow, net worth, investment analysis.

Financial Sense. Computer Language Research Inc. [Fast-Tax], 2395 Midway Road, Carrollton, TX 75006, 214-934-7000, available on a timesharing basis. Major features: income tax planning, income & cash flow, net worth, investment analysis. Batch computer service system. Tax numbers transferred direct by line# from 1040 on Fast-Tax system.

Finsystem. Tymshare, Inc., 639 North Euclid, Anaheim, CA 92801, 714-956-3640, 213-264-0500, available on a timesharing basis. Major

Adapted from a speech delivered to the American Institute of Certified Public Accountants by Martin J. Satinsky, Tax Partner, Coopers & Lybrand, Philadelphia, Pennsylvania. Used with permission.

features: income tax planning, income & cash flow, net worth, investment analysis. Time sharing service system.

IFDS Financial Planning Systems. International Financial Data Systems, Inc., 875 Johnson Ferry Road, Suite 220, Atlanta, GA 30342, 404-256-6447, 800-554-8004, $8,000 - $15,000. Major features: income tax planning, income & cash flow, net worth, investment analysis.

Income Tax Spreadsheet. BNA Software, 1231 25th Street, N.W., Washington, D.C. 20037, 202-452-2253, $495. Major features: income tax planning.

Investment Plan. Benefit Analysis, Inc., 996 Old Eagle School Road, Wayne, PA 19087, 800-223-3601, $800 - $1200. Major features: investment analysis, portfolio detail. Basic investment analysis — $800. With portfolio detail — $1,200.

Investment Strategist. XQ Software, Inc., 4357 Park Drive, Norcross, GA 30093, 404-923-2880, $237. Major features: investment analysis.

Investware. New England Management Services, Inc., 345 Whitney Avenue, New Haven, CT 06511, 203-787-3452, $795 -$2445. Major features: portfolio detail. Links with Lotus 1-2-3 and word processing. Other special features can be added to the base price of $795.

Leonard Financial Planning Systems. Leonard Financial Planning Systems, Inc., 4513 Creedmoor Road, P.O. Box 30365, Raleigh, NC 27622, 919-781-1451, 800-632-3044, $4,000 + . Major features: income tax planning, income & cash flow, net worth, investment analysis.

Lifeplan. Life-work Planning, 1267 Cook Avenue, Lakewood, OH 44107, 216-228-1890, $495. Major features: income & cash flow, net worth.

Model 1040. Success Management Consultants, 318 Surview Drive, Pacific Palisades, CA 90272, 213-454-8030, $195. Major features: income tax planning.

Moneycalc Plus. Money Tree Software, 760 SW Madison Avenue, Corvallis, OR 97333, 503-757-1114, 800-533-3914, $2,600. Major features: income tax planning, income & cash flow, net worth, investment analysis, portfolio detail. Template system for Visicalc or Lotus 1-2-3 computer worksheets.

MoneyPlan. Money Tree Software, 760 SW Madison Avenue, Corvallis, OR 97333, 503-757-1114, 800-533-3914, $4,000. Major features: income tax planning, income & cash flow, net worth, investment analysis, portfolio detail. Integrated database system.

Money Manager. The American College, 270 Bryn Mawr Avenue, P.O. Box 1400, Bryn Mawr, PA 19010, 215-896-4500, $95. Major features: income & cash flow, net worth, investment analysis, portfolio detail. Template system for Visicalc, Lotus 1-2-3, or Multiplan computer worksheets.

The Permanent Portfolio Analyzer. C.R. Hunter & Associates, Inc., 1527 Northwood Drive, Cincinnati, OH 45237, 513-761-9322, $295. Major features: portfolio detail. "Inflation-Proofer Tutor" — Explains long-term forecasting. Available for additional $25.

The Personal Connection (various programs). Financial Planning Software [Dun & Bradstreet Plan Services], 4517 N. Sterling Avenue, Peoria, IL 61615, 309-688-4095, 800-447-0683, $75 - $445. Major features: income & cash flow. Demonstration disk reviewed. Various estate planning, income planning, and insurance policy analysis programs available.

PFP. Advanced Micro Applications Corp., P.O. Box 1228, USU Post Office, Logan UT 84322, 801-753-4382, $179. Major features: income & cash flow, net worth.

Planman. Sterling Wentworth Corp., 2744 Aspen Circle, Salt Lake City, UT 84109, 800-752-6626, $4500 plus $200 per quarter. Major features: income tax planning, income & cash flow, net worth, investment analysis. Requires 5 megabyte hard disk drive. Also requires Wordstar word processing program.

Planmode & Taxmode. Sawhney Software, 888 Seventh Avenue, New York, NY 10106, 212-541-8020, $395. Major features: income tax planning. State modules available.

The Professional Planning System. Micro Planning Systems, 1499 Bayshore Highway, Suite 214, Burlingame, CA 94010, 415-692-0407, $695. Major features: income tax planning, income & cash flow, net worth, investment analysis.

Professional Tax Planner. Aardvark/McGraw Hill, 1020 North Broadway, Milwaukee, WI 53202, 414-225-7500, $350. Major features: income tax planning. Includes report of after-tax effects of proposed investment alternatives being considered.

Proplan. Financial Planning Consultants, Inc., The Financial Planning Building, 2507 N. Verity Parkway, Box 429, Middletown, OH 45042, 513-424-1656, 800-543-9252, $10,000. Major features: income tax planning, income & cash flow, net worth, investment analysis, portfolio detail.

Selfplan. Independence Strategies, 6631 Hazeltine #6, Van Nuys, CA 91405, 818-989-3012, $495. Major features: income tax planning, income & cash flow, net worth, investment analysis, portfolio detail.

Shorttax + Plus. Syntax Corporation, 4500 W. 72nd Terrace, Prairie Village, KS 66208, 913-362-9667, $295. Major features: income tax planning.

Softbridge Financial Planner. Softbridge Microsystems Corporation, 186 Alewife Brook Parkway, Cambridge, MA 02138, 617-576-2257, $4,000. Major features: income tax planning, income & cash flow, net worth, portfolio detail. Includes business valuation computations and estate planning.

Taxcalc. Taxcalc Software, Inc., 4210 W. Vickery Blvd., Fort Worth, TX 76107, 817-738-3122, $100. Major features: income tax planning. Template system for computer worksheets such as Lotus 1-2-3, Supercalc, Multiplan, etc. Other templates available.

Tax Planner Program. CPAids, Inc., 1061 Fraternity Circle, Kent OH 44240, 216-678-9015, $300. Major features: income tax planning.

Tax Relief. Micro Vision, 145 Wicks Road, Commack, NY 11725, 516-499-4010, $149 - $399 +. Major features: 1040 preparation. State returns available at additional cost.

Tax Strategist. XQ Software, Inc., 4357 Park Drive, Norcross, GA 30093, 404-923-2880, $237. Major features: income tax planning.

II

Discount Brokers Offering Services to Banks

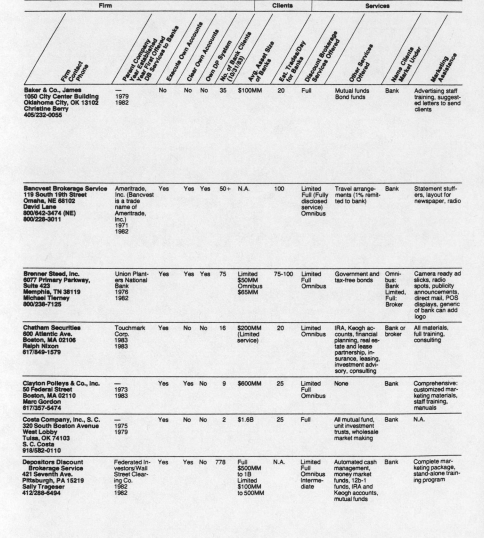

Firm								Clients			Services			
Firm Contact Phone	Parent Company	Year Established	Year First Offered DB Services to Banks	Execute Own Accounts	Clear Own Accounts	Own DP System	No. of Bank Clients (10/31/83)	Avg. Asset Size of Banks	Est. Trades/Day for Banks	Discount Brokerage Services Offered	Other Services Offered	Name Clients Market Under	Marketing Assistance
Baker & Co., James 1050 City Center Building Oklahoma City, OK 13102 Christine Berry 405/232-0055	—	1979	1982	No	No	No	35	$100MM	20	Full	Mutual funds Bond funds	Bank	Advertising staff training, suggested letters to send clients
Bancvest Brokerage Service 119 South 19th Street Omaha, NE 68102 David Lane 800/642-3474 (NE) 800/228-3011	Ameritrade, Inc. (Bancvest is a trade name of Ameritrade, Inc.) 1971 1982			Yes	Yes	Yes	50+	N.A.	100	Limited Full (Fully disclosed service) Omnibus	Travel arrangements (1% remitted to bank)	Bank	Statement stuffers, layout for newspaper, radio
Brenner Steed, Inc. 6077 Primary Parkway, Suite 423 Memphis, TN 38119 Michael Tierney 800/238-7125	Union Planters National Bank 1976 1982			Yes	Yes	Yes	75	Limited $50MM Omnibus $65MM	75-100	Limited Full Omnibus	Government and tax-free bonds	Omnibus: Bank Bank Limited, Full: Broker	Camera ready ad slicks, radio spots, publicity announcements, direct mail, POS displays, generic of bank can add logo
Chatham Securities 600 Atlantic Ave. Boston, MA 02106 Ralph Nixon 617/849-1579	Touchmark Corp. 1983 1983			Yes	No	No	16	$200MM (Limited service)	20	Limited Omnibus	IRA, Keogh accounts, financial planning, real estate and lease partnership, insurance, leasing, investment advisory, consulting	Bank or broker	All materials, full training, consulting
Clayton Polleys & Co., Inc. 50 Federal Street Boston, MA 02110 Marc Gordon 617/357-5474	— 1973 1983			Yes	Yes	No	9	$600MM	25	Limited Full Omnibus	None	Bank	Comprehensive: customized marketing materials, staff training, manuals
Costa Company, Inc., S. C. 320 South Boston Avenue West Lobby Tulsa, OK 74103 S. C. Costa 918/582-0110	— 1975 1979			Yes	No	No	2	$1.6B	25	Full	All mutual fund, unit investment trusts, wholesale market making	Bank	N.A.
Depositors Discount Brokerage Service 421 Seventh Ave. Pittsburgh, PA 15219 Sally Trageser 412/288-6494	Federated Investors/Wall Street Clearing Co. 1982 1982			Yes	Yes	No	778	Full $500MM to 1B Limited $100MM to 500MM	N.A.	Limited Full Omnibus Intermediate	Automated cash management, money market funds, 12b-1 funds, IRA and Keogh accounts, mutual funds	Bank	Complete marketing package, stand-alone training program

Adapted from an article by James F. Springfield, in *Bank Administration Institute*, Winter, 1984. Reprinted with permission.

		Costs				Contracts				
Settlement Transactions Delivered to Banks Computer-to-Computer	Up-Front Fees	Commission Rates % Broker's Bank	Special Service Charges	Revenue Checks Submitted	Length	Geographic Exclusivity	Broker Competes in Bank Markets	Nonproselytizing Clause	Bank Indemnified for Broker Processing Errors	Special Comments
No	None	See Special Comments	Accommodation transfers	Monthly	1-Year	No	No	N.A.	Yes	Banks decide what commission rate to charge. Most use 80% of 1975 rates, approximately 40% discount from full-service firms' rates. Commission split is 60/40 after transaction costs; if bank uses 1975 rates or above, 50/50. Firm takes orders from banks, sends out confirmations and handles all back-office work.
Yes	$5/MM assets, min. $500, max. $2,500	Min. $35 plus: .3%-.5% dollar value, min. 4¢/share, max. 45¢/ share stocks; .7%-.9% dollar value, min. $3/contract, max. $25/contract options; $3/bond Full: 72-80/20-28 Limited: 30-40/60-70 (Fully disclosed) Omnibus: Special arrangements	Special registration, delivery of certificates, legal items, accommodation transfers Rule 144 stock	Monthly	3-Year	No	Yes	Yes	Yes	Offer special promotions.
No	None	Limited and full: $35 + .004-.002 depending on $ amount; Omnibus 80% of limited-full service rates Limited and full: 80/20	Special registration, legal items, accommodation transfers	Monthly	1-Year	Negotiable	No	Yes	Yes	"First broker dealer to be purchased by a bank since 1933."
No	$2,500	Q&R schedule Limited: 80/20 (over 2,500 trades)	None	Monthly	2-Year	Usually	Usually not	Yes	Yes	
Yes	$1,000 initiation	Competitive rates Full: (negotiable) Limited: 70/30 Omnibus: 70/30	None	Monthly	1-3 Year	Negotiable	No	Yes	Yes	
No	None	Approx. 60% off old fixed rates Full 70/30	Legal items	Monthly	Varies	No	Yes	No	Yes	
No	None	Stocks: rates depend on dollar amounts, min. $37.50/trade, max. $.45/share; Bonds: $25 + $3/ bond, 25th bond and over + $2/bond, min. $37.50/order; Options: rates depend on dollar amounts, min. $37.50/order, max. $2.50/contract. Full: 85/15 min. Limited: 85/15 min. Omnibus: Clearing fee	Legal items, accommodation transfers, Rule 144 stock $30	Monthly	1-Year	No	No	·Yes	Yes	Bank employees are responsible for their processing errors or trading errors.

Discount Brokers continued

Firm (Firm Contact Phone)	Parent Company	Year Established	Year First Offered DB Service to Banks	Execute Own Accounts	Clear Own Accounts	Own DP System	No. of Bank Clients (10/31/83)	Avg. Asset Size of Banks	Est. Trades/Day for Banks	Discount Brokerage Services Offered	Other Services Offered	Name Clients Market Under	Marketing Assistance
Dis-Com Securities Inc. 1725 E. Hallandale Beach Blvd. Hallandale, FL 33009 Stuart M. Wolf or Brian Tarasuk 305/454-9800	First Union Corp. 1975 1983			No	No	No	Currently None	N.A.	N.A.	Limited Omnibus	Municipal, corporate and government bonds, unit trusts, mutual funds	N.A.	Advertising materials: newspaper ads, radio spots, yellow-page copy, direct marketing materials, press releases and various POS materials
Dominick & Dominick, Inc. 90 Broad Street New York, NY 10004 John J. Kennedy, Caroline M. Calder or Marcia A. Maher 212/558-8800	Dominick International Corp. 1870 1982			Yes	Yes	No	N.A.	N.A.	N.A.	Omnibus	Full-service investment banking firm	Bank	Work with clients individually
Estes & Company, Inc., W. N. 421 Union Street Nashville, TN 37219 Howell H. Campbell III 615/256-3656	— 1933 1979			No	No	No	2	N.A.	N.A.	Full	All general securities products	Bank or broker	None
Exchange Services, Inc. P.O. Box 7471 Richmond, VA 23221 Patteson Branch 804/798-1391	— 1978 1983			Yes	Yes	Yes	1	$15MM	500 trades/day capacity, can increase to 1,000 trades/day	Full (except margin A/C's and options) Omnibus	None	Bank/broker (joint)	Staff training
Financial Institution Clearing Services 199 West Palmetto Park Road Boca Raton, FL 33432 W. Dennis Ferguson 305/391-8897	Alan Bush Brokerage Co. 1975 1983			Yes	Yes	Yes	14	N.A.	60	Limited Full (Fully disclosed) Omnibus	Municipal bond trading, syndicate, corporate underwriting, corporate finance, unit trust, limited partnership (direct participation), research, commercial real estate	Bank or broker	Staff selection, development of department and brochures, advertising, speakers bureau, municipal, government, corporate and research weekly brochures
Financial Investors Securities Corp. 5801 North Broadway Suite 115 Oklahoma City, OK 73118 Mel James or Barbara Shane 405/843-1993	Adams, James, Foor & Co., Inc. and Trust Co. of Oklahoma 1983 1983			No	No	No	Non-operational	$100MM to $200MM	25	Full	Municipal bond evaluation and recommendations for Oklahoma dual exempt	Bank or broker	Advertising assistance, marketing plans
First Affiliated Securities, Inc. 6970 Miramar Road San Diego, CA 92121 Jack Alexander 619/578-9030	American First Corp. 1975 1983			No	No	No	30	$200MM	50	Full	Tax shelter underwritings, financial planning	Bank	Suggestions for advertising, staff
First Birmingham Securities Corp. 1200 Bank For Savings Building Birmingham, AL 35203 Ray Daffron 205/328-2666	— 1974 —			No	No	Yes	None	N.A.	N.A.	Full Omnibus	Bonds, government securities	Bank	Full-service marketing and sales training
Heartland Securities Inc. 208 South LaSalle Chicago, IL 60604 Charles A. Guptil 312/372-0075	— 1977 1983			Yes	Yes	No	1	Full $500MM Limited $500MM	3	Limited Omnibus	Stock, corporate bonds, options	Bank or broker	None
Hummer & Co., Wayne 175 West Jackson Boulevard Chicago, IL 60604 Philip Hummer 312/431-1700	— 1931 1984			Yes	Yes	No	N.A.	N.A.	N.A.	Limited	Full investment services	Broker	Advertisements, statement stuffers

Settlement Transactions Delivered to Banks Computer-to-Computer	Up-Front Fees	Commission Rates % Broker's/Bank	Special Service Charges	Revenue Checks Submitted	Length	Geographic Exclusivity	Broker Competes in Bank Markets	Nonproselytizing Clause	Bank Indemnified for Broker Processing Errors	Special Comments
No	Variable	N.A.	Legal items	Monthly	1-Year	Negotiable	Yes, in NC and FL	Upon request	Yes	
Yes	None	See Special Comments	None	Negotiable	90-days	"If mutually beneficial"	N.A.	No	Yes	"Bank selects its own commission schedule and broker charges are low."
Yes	None	Varies: Min. $35 Full 65/35	Special registration, legal items, accommodation transfers, Rule 144 stock	Monthly	N.A.	N.A.	Yes	N.A.	Yes	
Yes	$3,000 to $10,000 depending on bank size	$12.50/100 shares or ½ 1975 NYSE minimum commission, whichever is less; min. comm. $18.75 Full: 80/20 Limited and omnibus: negotiable	Duplicate confirmation, duplicate statements, special registration, safekeeping, delivery of certificates, legal items, accommodation transfers, Rule 144 stock	At bank request	1-Year	Negotiable	Yes	Yes	Yes, VA, CT, NY, NJ, PA, DE, MD, WV, NC, SC, GA, AL and FL	
Yes	None	Full: ticket charge $16 Limited: 70/30 Omnibus: ticket charge $14	Safekeeping, legal items, accommodation transfers	Monthly	1-Year	Yes	Yes (In one instance)	Yes	Yes	
No	None	"Generally well below previous fixed rate"	Legal items, accommodation transfers, Rule 144 stock	Monthly	1-Year (cancellable on 30-day notice)	Negotiable	No	Yes	Yes	
Yes	None	Not fixed 85/15	None	Monthly	Open	Yes	Sometimes	Yes	Yes	
Yes	Negotiable	Negotiable	Duplicate confirmation, duplicate statements, special registration, legal items	Monthly	N.A.	Yes (Alabama)	No	Yes	No	
No	None	Negotiable	None	Daily	Negotiable	Yes	No	Yes	Yes	Serves small banks with one to 100 transactions a month that are not interested in installing hardware and training staff for more sophisticated bank-discount broker relationships.
Yes	None	Min. $35/order; Stocks $25 + .0084-.0036 depending on dollar amount, max. $.40/share; Bonds $25 + $3/bond, $2 25th bond and over; Options $25 + .012-.006 depending on dollar amount, min. $35 or $2.50/contract, whichever is greater Limited: 85/25	Accommodation transfers	Monthly	1-Year	No	Yes	No	No	Business conducted under the name, Bankers Discount Brokerage Service, a subsidiary of Wayne Hummer & Co.

Discount Brokers continued

Firm / Contact / Phone	Parent Company / Year Established / Year First Offered DP Services to Banks	Execute Own Accounts	Clear Own Accounts	Own DP System	No. of Bank Clients (10/31/83)	Avg. Asset Size of Banks	Est. Trades/Day for Banks	Discount Brokerage Services Offered	Other Services Offered	Name Clients Market Under	Marketing Assistance
Investors Access—Division of Tweedy Browne Clearing Corp. 67 Wall Street New York, NY 10005 Marc Beerman or David Grayson 212/943-5616	Discount Brokerage Corporation 1976 1983	Yes	Yes	No	100	Confidential	Confidential	Limited Omnibus	Cash, margin, option accounts	Bank	Complete marketing package, custom staff training
Kall & Co., Inc. 615 South Flower, Suite 1012 Los Angeles, CA 90017 J. David Kall 213/626-4221	— 1969 1982	Yes	Yes	No	9 banks 4 S&Ls	N.A.	N.A.	Limited Fully disclosed	Mutual funds, Ginnie Maes, municipal bonds, and other products	Bank	Marketing package with suggested ideas
Kennedy, Cabot & Co. 9465 Wilshire Boulevard Beverly Hills, CA 90212 David Paul Kane 213/550-0711	— 1960 1974	No	No	Yes	12	Full $500MM Limited (no size limit)	110	Full	Mutual funds, municipals	Broker	Advertising assistance for publications and TV, circulars
Kramer Securities Corp. P.O. Drawer 431456 Miami, FL 33143 Al Kramer 305/667-9922	Independent Corp. 1965 1977	Sometimes	No	No	N.A.	N.A.	N.A.	Limited Full	Retirement plans, tax shelters	Bank or broker	Varies
Lafferty, R. F. & Co. 50 Broad Street New York, NY 10004 Henry Hackel 212/269-6636 800/221-8514	— 1945 1975	Yes	No	No	5	$1B+	3-4	Full	None	Bank	N.A.
Liss, Tenner, & Goldberg Securities Corp. 470 Colfax Avenue Clifton, NY 07013 Stanley R. Goldberg, Paul E. Greenburg 201/778-7300	— 1976 1983	Yes (OTC) No (Registered floor broker)	No	Yes	30	$50MM to $7B	250	Limited Full	Municipal bonds, corporate bonds, government bonds, options, tax-exempt bond funds	Bank	Sales force, staff training on- and off-site, advertising and marketing assistance
National Financial Services 161 Devonshire Street Boston, MA 02110 Leon W. Kumpe 617/451-3764	Fidelity Brokerage Services, Inc. 1979 1981	Yes	No	Yes	400	Full $4B Limited $400MM	2,000-3,000	Limited Full Scanset option	Correspondent program for discount brokerage, mutual funds, self-directed IRA, combined statement software	Bank	Personal visit to develop marketing plan, generic marketing kit with camera-ready artwork, marketing workshops, on-going consulting by experienced marketing staff
Oberweis Securities, Inc. 841 North Lake Street Aurora, IL 60506 Nathan Steele 312/897-7100	— 1978 1982	Yes	No	Yes	8	Full $100MM Limited N.A.	12-20	Limited Full Omnibus	Self-directed IRA and Keogh plans	Bank or broker	Assistance available from two financial marketing firms
Olde Discount Brokerage Services Olde Building 735 Griswold Detroit, MI 48226 John C. Marsh 800/521-2222	— 1971 1983	Yes	Yes	Yes	60	Full over $100MM Limited under $200MM	N.A.	Limited Full Omnibus	N.A.	Bank	Advertising budget planning media placement, graphic design, copy writing, electronic media, direct mail; staff training in-house and on-site
Pacific Brokerage Services 8200 Wilshire Boulevard, Suite 314 Beverly Hills, CA 90211 Steven Wallace 213/653-7300	— 1976 1982	Yes	Yes	No	2 banks 1 cu	Full $300MM	20	Full Other	Clearance of trust activities and utilization of Depository Trust Co. facilities for handling of trust securities	Bank or broker	Brochures, forms, telephone capacity etc.
Peremel & Co., Inc. 1 North Charles Street, Suite 407 Baltimore, MD 21201 H. Peremel 301/539-7171	— 1974 1984	Sometimes-	No	No	None	N.A.	N.A.	Full	Tax-free bond units, mutual funds, tax shelter investments, cash management accounts	Bank or broker	Work with bank or S&L to market program

		Costs					Contracts			
Settlement Transactions Delivered to Banks Computer-to-Computer	Up-Front Fees	Commission Rates % Broker/% Bank	Special Service Charges	Revenue Checks Submitted	Length	Geographic Exclusivity	Broker Competes in Bank Markets	Nonproselytizing Clause	Bank Indemnified for Broker Processing Errors	Special Comments
Yes	None	Up to 80% off full-service rates Full: negotiable Limited: 70/30	Accommodation transfers, Rule 144 stock	Monthly	1-Year	No	Yes	No	Yes	Assumes all financial risk for bad debts, errors etc.
Yes	None	Limited: 75/25 Fully disclosed: negotiable	None	Monthly	N.A. (can be cancelled in 30 days)	No	No	Yes	Yes	
Yes	None	Up to 90% discount on stocks, bonds and options Full: 50/50	None	Monthly	1-Year	Yes	No	Yes	Yes	
Yes	None	Variable Negotiable	Accommodation transfers	Monthly	Negotiable	Negotiable	N.A.	N.A.	Yes	
Yes	None	50% of 1975 rate or $12.50/100— whichever is lower N.A. (split)	None	Monthly	N.A.	N.A.	N.A.	N.A.	Yes	
Yes	None	Min. $35/transaction; Stocks vary by no. of shares and dollar value; Options vary by number of contracts; Bonds $3.50-$2.50, negotiable over 200 bonds Full 50/50 Limited 75/25	Special registration, legal items, Rule 144 stocks (charges are pass through, not add-on)	Monthly	3-Year	Possibly	No	No	Yes	"True joint venture. Members of N.Y.S.E."
Yes	$2,000 set up for limited service and scanset options; $7,500 for full-service option	$16 + 10% (Full service) Full: 33/67 Limited: 80/20	Extensions, mailgrams, statement postage, credit checks	Monthly	3-Year	No	Yes	Yes	Yes	
Yes	Usually none	Full: 80/20 Limited: 80/20 Omnibus: 80/20	None	Monthly	Varies	Varies	Rarely	Yes	Yes	
Yes	None	Choice of 4 discount brokerage schedules Full (Phase 1) 75/25 Limited (Phase 2) $20 + 2¢/share 50/50 remainder Omnibus (Phase 3) $10 + 2¢/share 50/50 remainder	Special registration, delivery of certificates, legal items, accommodation transfers	Monthly	Depends on service	No	No	N.A.	Yes	
Yes	None	N.A.	Legal items, custom forms, printing, extraordinary clearing expenses and transfer fees	Monthly	1-Year renewable	No	Yes	Yes	Yes	
Yes	None	Up to 70% discount Negotiable	Negotiable	Monthly	Negotiable	No	Yes	Negotiable	Yes	

Discount Brokers *continued*

Firm / Contact / Phone	Parent Company / Year Established / Year Firm Offered DB Services to Banks	Execute Own Accounts	Clear Own Accounts	Own DP System	No. of Bank Clients (10/31/83)	Avg. Asset Size of Banks	Est. Trades/Day for Banks	Discount Brokerage Services Offered	Other Services Offered	Name Clients Market Under	Marketing Assistance
Pershing 141 West Jackson Boulevard Suite 825A Chicago, IL 60604 Barry Rundle 312/987-8130	Donaldson, Lufkin, & Jenrette 1939 1982	Yes	Yes	Yes	300+	Full $500MM Limited less than $500MM	1,250	Limited Omnibus Full Execution only	IRA, Keogh, SEP, block execution, research, family of money market funds, $2,500,000 insurance	Bank	Industry demographics and statistics
Portfolio Securities Transactions Corp. 1520 Ohio Savings Plaza Cleveland, OH 44114 John R. Wilson 216/241-1865	— 1965 1975	No	No	Yes	10	$2B	10	Full	Tax shelters	Broker	Advertising
Quick & Reilly Inc. 120 Wall Street New York, NY 10271 Pat Mercurio 212/587-1403	Quick & Reilly Group, Inc. 1975 1982	Yes	Yes	No	15	N.A.	N.A.	Limited Full	None	Bank	Quick & Reilly's expertise
Robinson Securities Div. John Dawson & Associates, Inc. 11 South LaSalle Street, #2150 Chicago, Illinois 60603 John H. Dawson 312/346-7557	— 1972 1977	Yes	Yes	No	2	$60MM	5	Limited Omnibus	Safekeeping, margin, IRA, Keogh, options, DVP, accommodation transfers, legal transfers, money markets	Bank or broker	Advertising agency resources
Salem Securities, Inc. P.O. Box 522 Winston-Salem, NC 27102 Clarence L. Fisher, Jr. 800/334-9406 (outside NC) 800/532-0367 (NC)	First Union Corporation N.A. 1983	Yes	No	No	20	Limited $20MM	50	Limited Full Relay	None	Bank	Newspaper slicks, radio spots, yellow page ads, direct mail letter, press releases, statement inserts, investor guides and other POS items
Security Pacific Brokers, Inc. 297 North Marengo Avenue Pasadena, CA 91101 Craig Madsen 213/304-3522	Security Pacific National Bank 1983 1983	Yes	Yes	No	199 Banks 6 S&Ls	N.A.	100	Limited	Trading in equities options, municipal and government bonds, self-directed IRAs	Bank	Complete implementation manual, marketing and positioning advice, generic advertising and POS promotional materials, or camera ready art, bank can customize, radio scripts, video training tapes, training handbooks and on-site training
Texas Securities, Inc. 815 Throckmorton, Suite 300 Fort Worth, TX 76102 Sara B. Jones 817/877-1191	— 1979 N.A.	Yes	No	Yes	0	N.A.	N.A.	Full	Commodities, bonds, options, tax shelters, limited partnerships	Bank or broker	Negotiable

Settlement Transactions Delivered to Banks Computer-to-Computer	Up-Front Fees	Costs				Contracts				
		Commission Rate % Broker/% Bank	Special Service Charges	Revenue Checks Submitted	Length	Geographic Exclusivity	Broker Competes in Bank Markets	Nonproselytizing Clause	Bank Indemnified for Broker Processing Errors	Special Comments
Yes	None	Client decides Full: 33/67 Limited: 70/30 Omnibus: 15/85	Legal items, accommodation transfers, Rule 144 stock, communications	Daily	1-Year, 90-day cancellation	No	No	Yes	Yes	
Yes	None	Negotiated Full 60/40	None	Monthly	Negotiable	Negotiable	No	Yes	Yes	
No	None	Approx. 50% off N.A.	None	Monthly	1-Year	No	Yes	Yes	N.A.	
Yes	None	Negotiable	Accommodation transfers	Monthly	No contract	N.A.	No	N.A.	Yes	
Yes	None	Sliding scale based on market price x no. of shares. First $25 to broker, remainder split 50/50	None	Monthly	1-Year	No	Only in NC	No	Yes	
Yes	None	$35 min. commission; Stocks $35 + .005-.003 depending on transaction $ amount, max. .45¢/share, min. 4¢/share; Options $35 + .009-.007 depending on transaction $ amount, max. $25/contract, min. $3/contract, Bonds $4/bond Limited: 85-80/15-20	None	Monthly	1-Year	No	Yes	Yes	Yes	Pioneered discount brokerage area, bank oriented, vertically integrated.
Yes	Negotiable	Customers get their own rates Split negotiable	None	Monthly	Negotiable	Yes	No	Yes	Yes	

III

Correspondent Banks Offering Discount Brokerage Services to Other Banks

	Correspondent Bank						Respondents					
Bank Contact Phone Parent Company	Have Offered Correspondent DP Services Since	Execute Own Accounts	Clear Own Accounts	Own DP System	Executing Broker		No. of Respondents (10/1/83)	Avg Asset Size of DB Respondents	Est. Trades/Day for Banks	Discount Brokerage Services Offered	Other Securities Related Products	Name Respondents Market Under
Alabama												
Central Bank of the South P.O. Box 10566 Birmingham, AL 35296 Sandra Little 205/933-3031 Central Bancshares of the South, Inc.	July 1983	No	No	No	Depositors Discount Brokerage Services (Federated)		16	$35MM	1	Limited	Asset-Liability management, public finance and bond dealer (taxable and tax-free) services.	Respondent
Southtrust Bank of Alabama, N.A. P.O. Box 2554 Birmingham, AL 35290 Bob Gray 205/254-5920 Southtrust Corp.	September 1983	No	No	No	Wall Street Clearing Co.		18	$100MM	3	Full	Full service.	Respondent
California												
Union Bank (Market Investment Services) 445 S. Figueroa Street Los Angeles, CA 90071 Elizabeth J. Fisher 213/236-7919 Standard Chartered-London	November 1983	No	No	No	National Financial Services Corp. (Fidelity)		N.A.	N.A.	N.A.	Limited Omnibus	Complete fixed income package.	Respondent
Delaware												
Wilmington Trust P.O. Box 8988 Wilmington, DE 19899 Sheldon M. Frank 302/651-1011	March 1983	No	No	No	National Financial Services Corp. (Fidelity)		6	$375MM	12-15	Limited	Mutual funds, gold and silver.	Respondent
Florida												
Southeast Bank, N.A. P.O. Box 012500 Miami, FL 33101 Hershel F. Smith, Jr. Aletha S. Connors 305/577-4800	June 1983	Yes	No	No	National Financial Services Corp. (Fidelity)		6	N.A.	5	Full	N.A.	Respondent
Georgia												
Bank South 55 Marietta Street Atlanta, GA 30303 Katie McLendon 404/529-4178 Bank South Corporation	March 1983	Yes	No	No	Pershing & Co.		10	N.A.	N.A.	Limited	Stocks, corporate bonds, equity options and margin trading.	Correspondent*

Adapted from an article by James F. Springfield, in *Bank Administration Institute*, Winter, 1984. Reprinted with permission.

Services			Costs				Contracts		
Marketing Assistance	Settlement Transactions Delivered to Banks Computer-to-Computer	Up-Front Fees	Commission Rates % Correspondent/ % Respondent	Special Service Charges	Revenue Checks Submitted	Length	Geographic Exclusivity	Indemnify Respondents for Correspondent Processing Errors	Special Comments
Copies of all marketing material with suggestions for what has been successful.	Yes	None	Under 5M, 1.5% 5M to 15M, 1.2% 15M to 50M, .8% Over 50M, .5% Limited: 35% gross commission to respondent.	Legal items Rule 144 stock	Monthly	1-Year	N.A.	Yes	
Brochures, newspaper, direct mail.	No	None	$27.50 plus: stocks .0092-.0040 of $ amount depending on transaction volume; Options .013-.007 of $ amount depending on transaction volume; Corp. Bonds $3.30/bond-$2.20/bond, min. $38.50. Full: $5 or 8% (whichever is greater)/17% (gross commission).	Registered mailing fee	Monthly	No contract	N.A. Alabama	Yes	Southtrust supplies discount brokerage service only to its affiliate banks. It plans to offer service to nonaffiliates on a correspondent basis in future, at which time commission splits will be established.
Generic literature kit (camera ready) plus on-going assistance.	No	None	N.A. Limited: 80/20 Omnibus: 80/20	None	Monthly	No time frame	No	Yes	
Art for custom brochures and applications, also for advertisements.	No	None	Varies with size of institution. Up to 25% of gross commission to respondent.	None	Monthly	2-Year	Negotiable	Yes	
Total marketing assistance.	Yes	$2,000	Stocks $35 + .008-.004 of $ amount, min. charge $40/transaction; Options $35 + .013-.009 of $ amount; Corporate bonds $35 + $4.50-$2.50/bond; Margin accounts 2%-¼% over broker's call money rate. Full: 85/15	None	Monthly	Unlimited	No	Yes	
All marketing materials currently used by corporation and brokerage service department.	No	None	Stocks $35 + .008-.0025 depending on $ amount; Options $35 + .009-.007 depending on $ amount; Corporate bonds margin accounts broker loan rate + 2¼%-1% surcharge based on net debit balance. % commission split based on per annum accrual and escalates.	None	Monthly	Open-end	No	Yes	At time of preparation, marketing under correspondent name was targeted for January 1984. Settlement to respondent customer is not direct since correspondent does not require respondent customers to open settlement accounts at Bank South. Therefore respondent makes bookkeeping entries at their bank.

Correspondent Banks continued

Bank Contact Phone Parent Company	Have Offered Corres. DP Services Since	Execute Own Accounts	Clear Own Accounts	Own DP System	Executing Broker	No. of Respondents (10/1/83)	Avg. Asset Size of DB Respondents	Est. Trades/Day for Banks	Discount Brokerage Services Offered	Other Securities Related Products	Name Respondents Market Under
Correspondent Bank						**Respondents**					
Kansas											
Fourth National Bank & Trust Co. P.O. Box 1090 Wichita, KS 67201 Margaret E. Hornbeck 316/261-4213 Fourth Financial Corp.	March 1983	No	No	No	Depositors Discount Brokerage Service (Federated)	16	$20MM	2	Full	Municipal bonds, commercial paper, repos governments, agencies, B.A.'s.	Respondent
Kentucky											
Liberty National Bank & Trust Co. P.O. Box 32500 Louisville, KY 40232 Elisabeth Y. Clark 502/566-2406 Liberty United Bancorp.	September 1983	No	No	No	Pershing & Co.	13	$100MM	5	Limited Full	Dealer in governments, agencies, and municipals, full-service trust department.	Respondent
Massachusetts											
Shawmut Bank of Boston, N.A. One Federal Street Boston, MA 02211 Peter N. Dana 617/292-2178 Shawmut Corporation	N.A.	No	No	No	National Financial Services Corp. (Fidelity)	N.A.	$25MM	N.A.	Limited	None presently through brokerage, have full-line investment division.	Respondent
Michigan											
Comerica Bank 211 West Fort Street Detroit, MI 48226 John Conway, IV 313/222-9554 Comerica, Inc.	November 1983	No	No	No	National Financial Services Corp. (Fidelity)	5	$100MM	5	Limited	Discount investment advice, self-directed IRA, precious metals, municipal bonds, commercial paper, treasury instrument.	Respondent
Manufacturers National Bank of Detroit 411 West Lafayette Detroit, MI 48226 Larry C. Kreul 313/222-3252 Manufacturers National Corp.	May 1983	No	No	No	Pershing & Co.	7	$100MM	35	Limited	Government securities, municipal securities, self-directed IRA.	Correspondent "Advantage Investment Service"
Missouri											
Commerce Bank of Kansas City, N.A. P.O. Box 529 Kansas City, MO 64141 William R. Salmonson 816/234-2440 Commerce Bancshares	April 1983	No	No	No	National Financial Services Corp. (Fidelity)	N.A.	N.A.	N.A.	Limited Omnibus	N.A.	Respondent
Centerre Bank, N.A. 1 Centerre Plaza St. Louis, MO 63102 Karen A. McClure 800/453-8888 (Outside Missouri) 800/252-2222 (Missouri) Centerre Bancorp.	June 1983	No	No	No	Pershing & Co.	39	$ 50-$100MM	20	Limited Full Omnibus	Government and municipal bonds.	Respondent
Mercantile Trust Company, N.A. P.O. Box 387 St. Louis, MO 63166 Timothy S. Engelbrecht Rosemary Takacs 314/425-2692 314/425-2708 Mercantile Bancorp.	To be offered	Yes	Yes	No	N.A.	0	N.A.	N.A.	Omnibus	Investment research and advisory services, security settlement service, financial planning software, tax shelter consulting service.	Correspondent
New Jersey											
New Jersey National Bank 370 Scotch Road Trenton, NJ 08648 James R. Booth 609/771-5850 New Jersey National Corporation	November 1982	No	No	No	N.A.	3	$75MM	5	Full	U.S. Treasury & agency, municipal notes and bonds, money market instruments.	Correspondent

Services			Costs				Contracts		
Marketing Assistance	Settlement Transactions Delivered to Banks/Computer-to-Computer	Up-Front Fees	Commission Rates % Correspondent/% Respondent	Special Service Charges	Revenue Checks Submitted	Length	Geographic Exclusivity	Indemnify Respondents for Correspondent Processing Errors	Special Comments
Staff training, user manuals, no marketing materials, but advice on design and production of such materials.	No	None	Stocks $30 + .0101-.0043 of $ amount, min. $42, max. 48¢/share; Corporate bonds $30 + $3.60-$240/bond, min. $42, no max. Full: 90/10	Accommodation transfers	Monthly	No term	No	Yes	
Brochures and application forms, either generic or customized, generic internal forms, sample ads, letters, press releases.	No	None	At discretion of respondent. Full: 25% + up to 10% with volume to respondent. Limited: 15% + up to 10% with volume to respondent.	Accommodation transfers, Rule 144 stock	Monthly, weekly or daily	60-day	No	Yes	
Staff training, sample literature, manuals, etc.	Yes	None	"Same as ours." N.A.	Special registration, Safekeeping	Monthly	1-Year renewable	Occasionally	Yes	
At cost, brochures, statement stuffers, countercards, newspaper ads, press releases, radio copy, assistance in tailoring own marketing program.	Yes	None	Up to 70% off pre-May day rates. "Same rates as our own customers." Limited: 25% of gross commissions over $45 goes to respondent.	Special registration	Monthly	2-Year	No	Yes	Implementation 45 days or less. Indepth training, complete training manuals at no cost. Makes variety of product extensions (e.g., self-directed IRAs) available to respondents.
Statement stuffers, lobby rack brochures, direct mail promotion prospect research.	Yes	None	Less than $15,000 comm. = .005 + $35, $15,001-$50,000 comm. = .004 + $35, + $50,000 comm. = .003 + $35 Limited: 85/15	Delivery of certificates, Accommodation transfers	Monthly	Indefinite with immediate cancel rights	No	Yes	
Commercial marketing department.	Yes	$100-150 + materials	Stocks $35 + .008-.003 of $ amount; Options $35 + .011-.007 of $ amount; Bonds $35 + $4-$3/bond; margin rates 2%-¼% depending on debit balance. Limited: 60/40 Omnibus: 60/40	Special registration	Monthly	Cancellable anytime	No	Yes	
Advertising copy.	No	None	N.A. Limited: 85/15 Full: 75/25 Omnibus: 85/15	Legal items, Accommodation transfers	Monthly	30-day cancellation	No	Yes	
Not yet determined.	No (unless D.T.C. Piggyback client)	Not yet determined	Negotiated with respondents based on volume.	None	Monthly	1-Year	No	Yes	
Samples of advertising literature-brochures, ads, stuffers.	Yes	None	Varying percentage (.005-.003 of proceeds + $35). Full: 75/25	Special registration, Accommodation transfers	Monthly	2-Year	No	Yes	

Correspondent Banks continued

	Correspondent Bank					Respondents					
Bank / Contact / Phone / Parent Company	Have Offered Corres. DP Services Since	Execute Own Accounts	Clear Own Accounts	Own DP System	Executing Broker	No. of Respondents (10/1/83)	Avg. Asset Size of DB Respondents	Est. Trades/Day for Banks	Discount Brokerage Services Offered	Other Securities Related Products	Name Respondents Market Under
New Mexico											
First National Bank in Albuquerque P.O. Box 1305 Albuquerque, NM 87103 Paula Rodgers 505/765-4500	December 1982	No	No	No	SEI Financial Services	0	N.A.	N.A.	N.A.	Not determined at this time.	Respondent
New York											
Marine Midland Bank, N.A. One Marine Midland Center Buffalo, NY 14240 Wallace Grieser 716/843-4651 Marine Midland Banks, Inc.	September 1983	Yes	No	No	Pershing & Co.	N.A.	$2B	N.A.	Limited	Safekeeping, custody.	Respondent
Lincoln First Bank, N.A. One Lincoln First Square Rochester, NY 14614 Ray Mack 716/258-6881 Lincoln First Banks, Inc.	N.A.	N.A.	N.A.	N.A.	National Financial Services Corp. (Fidelity)	N.A.	N.A.	N.A.	N.A.	N.A.	N.A.
North Carolina											
United Carolina Bank P.O. Box 632 Whiteville, NC 28472 Sherry Hooks 919/642-5131 United Carolina Bancshares Corp.	February 1983	No	No	No	Pershing & Co.	11	N.A.	N.A.	Full	Self Directed IRA	Correspondent
Wachovia Bank & Trust Co., N.A. P.O. Box 3075 Winston-Salem, NC 27102 Ellen S. Sartin 919/748-6531 The Wachovia Corp.	1st quarter 1984	No	No	Yes	Execution Service Inc.	N.A.	N.A.	N.A.	Limited	Securities custody.	Correspondent Respondent
Ohio											
First National Bank of Cincinnati 425 Walnut Street Cincinnati, OH 45202 Cassandra Middleton Timothy J. Sheridan 513/632-4000 First National Cincinnati Corp.	November 1983	No	No	No	Dominick Investor Service Corp.	None	N.A.	N.A.	Omnibus	N.A.	Respondent
AmeriTrust Corporation 900 Euclid Avenue Cleveland, OH 44101 Merryl K. Rapp 216/687-2924 AmeriTrust Corporation	Early 1984	No	No	Yes	National Financial Services Corp. (Fidelity)	N.A.	$5MM to $1B	N.A.	Limited	N.A.	Correspondent
Oklahoma											
First National Bank and Trust Company P.O. Box 25189 Oklahoma City, OK 73125 Trisha Hedlock 405/272-4604 First Oklahoma Bancorp.	July 1983	No	No	No	A. G. Becker	20	$50MM	20	Limited	N.A.	Respondent
Pennsylvania											
First Pennsylvania Bank N.A. First Pennsylvania Discount Brokerage Services P.O. Box 13669 Philadelphia, PA 19101 Robert R. DeLong, Jr. 215/786-8500 First Pennsylvania Corp.	May 1983	Yes	No	No	National Financial Services Corp. (Fidelity)	4,815	$75MM	N.A.	Full	N.A.	Correspondent

| Services | | | Costs | | | | Contracts | | |
Marketing Assistance	Settlement Transactions Delivered to Banks Computer-to-Computer	Up-Front Fees	Commission Rates % Correspondent/ % Respondent	Special Service Charges	Revenue Checks Submitted	Length	Geographic Exclusivity	Indemnify Respondent for Correspondent Processing Errors	Special Comments
Provide marketing material for respondents to reprint with their own names and logos.	No	Not determined at this time	Not established.	Not established	Monthly	N.A.	Yes	Yes	
Generic ads, direct mail and display material, camera ready art.	Yes	$1,500	Retail $40 + 20¢/share over 100 shares; 25% rebate to respondent. Limited: 75/25	None	Monthly	Open-ended, 90-day cancellation	By special amendment	Yes	
N.A.	N.A.	N.A.	N.A.	N.A.	N.A.	N.A.	N.A.	N.A.	
Samples for brochures, newspaper ads, statement stuffers, direct mail, radio spots. Provide staff training, user manuals, printing assistance.	Yes	None	N.A. Full: 60/40	Legal items	Monthly	30-day cancellation	No	Yes	
Training, implementation package, newspaper ads, in-lobby materials and display, new account materials.	Yes	N.A.	Under development.	Duplicate confirmation, Duplicate statements, Special registration, Safekeeping, Legal items, Accommodation transfers, Rule 144 stock	Monthly	Negotiable	No	Yes	Margin lending program structured under Reg. U, funded through bank.
Generic radio spots, newspaper ads, statement stuffers and brochures.	No	None	Under $5M: $28 + .008 on $ amount. $5-15M: $28 + .006 on $ amount. $15-25M: $28 + .005 on $ amount. $25-50M: $28 + .004 on $ amount. Over $50M: $28 + .003 on $ amount. Omnibus: 70/30	N.A.	Monthly	Open-ended	No	Yes	
Generic lobby literature, lobby signs, customer handbook, newspaper ads, direct mail.	No	N.A.	N.A.	Legal items	Monthly	N.A.	No	Yes	
Newspaper ads, brochures, training.	No	None	20% Limited: 80/20	Accommodation	Monthly	1-Year	Yes	No	
N.A.	No	N.A.	$30+: Stocks .005-.003 of $ amount, min. 4¢/share, max. 45¢/share; Options .009-.007 of $ amount, min. $3/contract, max. $25/contract; Bonds $3/$1,000 bond. Negotiable	Special registration	Monthly	1-Year	N.A.	N.A.	

Correspondent Banks continued

	Correspondent Bank					Respondents					
Bank / Contact / Phone / Parent Company	Have Offered Corres. DP Services Since	Execute Own Accounts	Clear Own Accounts	Own DP System	Executing Broker	No. of Respondents (10/1/83)	Avg. Asset Size of DB Respondents	Est. Trades/Day for Banks	Discount Brokerage Services Offered	Other Securities Related Products	Name Respondents Market Under
Provident National Bank Broad and Chestnut Sts. Philadelphia, PA 19101 Thomas K. Whitford 215/585-5468 PNC Financial Corp.	January 1984	Yes	Yes	Yes	N.A.	N.A.	N.A.	N.A.	Limited Full	Institutional investment service.	Respondent
Equibank Two Oliver Plaza— 12th Floor Pittsburgh, PA 15222 David I. Chijner 412/288-5700 Equimark Corporation	June 1983	No	No	No	National Financial Services Corp. (Fidelity)	26	$60MM	3-5	Limited	Stocks, options, corporate bonds.	Correspondent
Pittsburgh National Bank Fifth Ave. & Wood St. Pittsburgh, PA 15222 A. Richard Markson 412/355-3979 PNCF	October 1983	No	No	No	National Financial Services Corp. (Fidelity)	6	$2B	N.A.	Full Omnibus	None	Correspondent
American Bank and Trust Co. 35 North 6th Street Reading, PA 19603 Karen E. Loessi 215/320-3216 Meridian Bancorp.	September 1983	Yes	No	No	Q & R Clearing Corp.	None	$1B	N.A.	Full	Trust accounts, re-registration of securities, central asset accounts.	Correspondent
Rhode Island											
Fleet National Bank 111 Westminster Street Providence, RI 02903 Frederick W. Sackett 401/278-6900 Fleet Financial Group	September 1983	Yes	No	Yes	National Financial Services Corp. (Fidelity)	None	N.A.	N.A.	Limited	IRA, mutual funds.	Correspondent (Generic name)
South Carolina											
Citizens & Southern National Bank C&S Discount Brokerage P.O. Box 22200 Columbia, SC 29222 Nanda Reed 803/765-8489 Citizens & Southern Corp.	N.A.	N.A.	N.A.	N.A.	National Financial Services Corp. (Fidelity)	None	N.A.	N.A.	N.A.	N.A.	N.A.
First National Bank of South Carolina P.O. Box 111 Columbia, SC 29202 Ronald C. Paxton, Jr. 803/771-3957 First Bankshares Corp.	September 1983	No	No	No	National Financial Services Corp. (Fidelity)	3	$30-50MM	N.A.	Limited	Bond department handles munis, governments and agencies for respondents.	Correspondent (Brokerage department trade name)
South Carolina National Bank Discount Brokerage Service 101 Greystone Boulevard Columbia, SC 29226 Frank Chapman David Hutchison 803/765-3549 South Carolina National Corp.	July 1983	Yes	No	No	National Financial Services Corp. (Fidelity)	15	Small-medium	Varies	Limited	Self-directed IRA.	Respondent
Tennessee											
First Tennessee Bank P.O. Box 84 Memphis, TN 38101 Paul Mann 901/523-5900 800/238-1111 First Tennessee National Corp.	July 1982	No	No	Yes	National Financial Services Corp. (Fidelity)	81	$2MM	14	Full	None	Respondent

Services				Costs				Contracts		
Marketing Assistance	Settlement Transactions Delivered to Banks Computer-to-Computer	Up-Front Fees	Commission Rates % Correspondent/ % Respondent	Special Service Charges	Revenue Checks Submitted	Length	Geographic Exclusivity	Indemnify Respondents for Correspondent Processing Errors	Special Comments
Marketing planning, sample promotional material, training manual.	N.A.	None	N.A.	Duplicate statements, Special registration, Legal items, Accommodation transfers	Monthly	1-Year	N.A.	Yes	
Statement stuffers, lobby posters, sample newspaper ads and radio spots.	No	None	Stocks $35 + .005-.003 of $ amount, max. 45¢/share. min. 4¢/share; Options $35 + .009-.007 of $ amount, max. $25/contract, min. $3/ contract; Bonds $30 + $3/ $1,000 bond. N.A.	None	Monthly	1-Year	No	Yes	
Complete.	No	None	N.A. Full: 80/20 Omnibus: 80/20	None	Monthly	"Their choice"	No	Yes	
Advertising copy.	No	None	35-70% off old NYSE fixed commission rates; $34 minimum. Full: 80/20	Special registration	Monthly	1-Year	No	Yes	
Package containing correspondent's advertising as well as that of competitors, consultation case by case.	N.A.	None	Stocks, under $1,000, $30 + .006 of $ amount, over $1,000, $35 + .005-.003 of $ amount; Options, under $1,000, $30 + .01 of $ amount, over $1,000, $35 + .009-.007 of $ amount; Corporate Bonds, $30 + $3/bond. Limited: 80/20	Accommodation transfers	Monthly	1-Year	No	Yes	
N.A.	N.A.	N.A.	N.A.	N.A.	N.A.	N.A.	N.A.	N.A.	"We have not established procedures because we have not found interest among respondent banks. We would like to offer the service."
Marketing brochures and flyers for direct use of guidance. Marketing dept. rep. available to answer questions.	Yes	None	Stocks $30 + .008-.003 $ transaction amount, max. 45¢/share, min. 5¢/share; Bonds $30 + $4-$3/bond; Options $30 + .012-.007 $ transaction amount, max. $25/contract, min. $3/ contract. Limited: 85/15	Accommodation transfers	Monthly	1-Year renewable thereafter	No	Yes	
Varies.	No	None	N.A. 75/25	Special registration Rule 144 stock	Monthly	Variable	No (nego- tiable)	Yes	
Ad slicks.	N.A.	None	Stocks $35 + 5%-3% of transaction amount, max. 45¢/share, min. 4¢/share; Options $35 + .9%-.7% of transaction amount, max. $25/contract, min. $3/con- tract; Bonds $30 + $3/ bond, $35 min. Full: 80/20	None	Monthly	1-Year	No	Yes	

Correspondent Banks continued

	Bank Contact Phone Parent Company	Have Offered Corres. DB Services Since	Execute Own Accounts	Clear Own Accounts	Own DP System	Executing Broker	No. of Respondents (10/1/83)	Avg. Asset Size of DB Respondents	Est. Trades/Day for Banks	Discount Brokerage Services Offered	Other Securities Related Products	Name Respondents Market Under
Correspondent Bank							**Respondents**					
Texas												
	Texas American Bank Fort Worth, N.A. P.O. Box 2050 Fort Worth, TX 76113 Jeff Moore 817/338-8288 Texas American Bancshares, Inc.	July 1983	Yes	No	No	National Financial Services Corp. (Fidelity)	26	$100MM	10	Limited	IRA accounts, margin lending.	Correspondent
	Frost National Bank P.O. Box 1600 San Antonio, TX 78296 Anita Hughes 512/220-4149 Cullen/Frost Bankers, Inc.	May 1983	Yes	No	No	National Financial Services Corp. (Fidelity)	26	$78MM	10	Limited	Securities trading in governments, commercial paper, repos—securities clearance, safekeeping, collection.	Correspondent
Virginia												
	Sovran Bank, N.A. P.O. Box 600 Norfolk, VA 23510 Jim LaVier 804/446-3585 Sovran Financial Corp.	June 1983	No	No	No	Pershing & Co.	15	$150MM	15	Limited	Government securities, municipal bonds, precious metals.	Respondent
	Dominion Bank P.O. Box 13327 Roanoke, VA 24040 Michael T. Morrisott 703/563-6347 Dominion Bankshares	N.A.	No	No	Yes	Bradford Brokerage Services	1	N.A.	N.A.	Full	Municipal bond sales, options.	Respondent
Washington												
	Old National Bank of Washington Suite 600 1111 3rd Avenue Seattle, WA 98101 Garry R. Arseneault 206/447-7373 Old National Bancorp.	June 1983	No	No	No	Pershing & Co.	2	$54MM	1	Limited	Precious metals, tax-exempt municipal bond fund, municipal bonds, U.S. Government securities.	Respondent
Wisconsin												
	First Wisconsin National Bank/Elanco Financial Services P.O. Box 2066 Milwaukee, WI 53201 George Krug 414/765-4386 First Wisconsin Corp.	March 1983	No	No	No	Pershing & Co.	180	$50-500MM	50	Limited Full (developing) Omnibus	Full trading capabilities for stock, bond and option trading for individuals, corporations, investment clubs and trusts; self-directed IRAs, (optional) municipal bond and treasury bill trading (optional).	Respondent plus correspondent trade name
	Marine Bank, N.A. 111 East Wisconsin Ave. P.O. Box 974 Milwaukee, WI 53201 Krien VerBerkmoes 414/765-2100 The Marine Corporation	June 1983	No	No	No	National Financial Services Corp. (Fidelity)	28	N.A.	N.A.	Full	None	Correspondent

Services			Costs				Contracts		
Marketing Assistance	Settlement Transactions Delivered to Banks Computer-to-Computer	Up-Front Fees	Commission Rates % Correspondent/ % Respondent	Special Service Charges	Revenue Checks Submitted	Length	Geographic Exclusivity	Indemnity Respondents for Correspondent Processing Errors	Special Comments
Assist in developing detailed marketing program and strategy—designing literature, ordering forms, training employees.	No	None	Stocks $35 + .008-.003 of $ amount, max. 45¢/share, min. 4¢/share; Options $35 + .011-.007 of $ amount, max. $25/contract, min. $3/ contract; Bonds $30 + $4/bond. Limited: 85-80/15-20	None	Monthly	1-Year	No	Yes	
Statement inserts, sales brochures, Q & A brochures, commission schedules, newspaper and advertisements, lobby posters. May be customized with respondent's logo.	No	None	$30+: Stocks .008-.003 of $ amount, min. $30; Options .01-.008 of $ amount, min. $3/contract, max. $25/ contract; Bonds $3/$1,000 par. Full: 15%-$5M, 25%-$5M-$10M, 33⅓%-$10M+ to respondent.	Special registration, Accommodation transfers	Monthly	1-Year	No	Yes	
Consultation on marketing and staff training.	No	None	Stocks $25-$40 + 1%-.4% of $ amount depending on volume, max. charge 45¢/ share, min. $35; Bonds $5/$1,000 face value, min. $35. Limited: 80/20	Rule 144 stock	Monthly or quarterly	Negotiable	No	Yes	
Brochures, newspaper ads, POS display.	No	Negotiable	$35 + .4%-3%. Full: 80/20	None	Monthly	90-Day	Negotiable	Under contract	"We are rearranging the correspondent program. Some of the services might change."
Generic support materials including advertising.	Yes	None	$30+: Stocks .008-.003 of $ amount, min. $30 + 5¢/ share; Options .011-.007 of $ amount; Bonds $3/ $1,000 face value. Limited: 85-75/15-25	Accommodation transfers, Rule 144 stock	Monthly	No contract	N.A.	Yes	
Assist with marketing plans, provide statement inserts, print ad proofs, radio scripts, lobby posters, direct mail letter copy and list selection assistance. Complete training (videotape and personal), fully documented procedures manual and packaged forms kit.	Yes	None	$35+: 5¢-23¢/share depending on price/share and volume; Bonds $6-$3/bond depending on volume. Options $35-$362.66 depending on option price and volume. Full: N.A. Limited: 47/up to 20 Omnibus: 47/up to 20	Legal items, Accommodation transfers	Daily	1-Year	No	Yes	
One-third of media cost and up to 5% gross commission for first six months.	Yes	None	Min. $28 + max. 8% commission/transaction value. Full: 80/20	Special registration, Accommodation transfers	Monthly	1-Year	No	Yes	

IV

Market Research Firms

Allstate Research and Planning Center, 321 Middlefield Road, Menlo Park, CA 94025, 415-324-2721. Human resources service company. Analyzes minority employment market for affirmative action hiring programs.

Analysis and Forecasting, Inc., P.O. Box 415, Cambridge, MA 02138, 617-491-8171. Consulting services. Analyzes and projects national trends in household and family structure.

Biddle & Associates, 903 Enterprise Drive, Suite 1, Sacramento, CA 95825, 916-929-7670. Human resources service company. Specializes in equal opportunity training, consulting, and production of personnel software.

C.A.C.I., Inc., 1815 N. Fort Myer Drive, Arlington, VA 22209, 800-336-6600, 703-841-7807. General demographic/research service. SITE II presents 1980 census data, current year estimates, five-year forecasts. SITE POTENTIAL reports estimated consumer demand by household for more than 140 product lines. DORIS lets clients access census data to make their own reports. ACORN (C.A.C.I.'s cluster analysis system) labels block groups according to 44 different demographic/socioeconomic types.

California Survey Research, 15250 Ventura Blvd., Sherman Oaks, CA 91403, 818-986-9444. Consulting services. Specializes in demographic consulting for firms interested in the California market.

Center for Continuing Study of the California Economy, 610 University Avenue, Palo Alto, CA 94301, 415-321-8551. Specializes in projecting economic and demographic variables for California. California Center Data Base offers complete economic/demographic data for California and its counties starting from 1970.

Chase Econometrics, 150 Monument Road, Bala Cynwyd, PA 19004, 215-896-4714. Forecasting service company. Uses econometric modelling to forecast consumer demand and demographic characteristics.

Claritas Corporation, 1911 N. Fort Myer Drive, Arlington, VA 22209, 703-841-9200. General demographic/research service. PRIZM (cluster

Adapted from "When Product Delivery Just Isn't Enough," by Mary E. Lubert, reprinted with permission of *American Banker,* October 22, 1984, p. 41 ff.

analysis system) assigns census tracts/zip codes a lifetime classification based on demographic data and buying patterns. THE CENSUS STORE offers census data on diskettes down to block group level.

Comerc Systems, 150 Executive Park Blvd., San Francisco, CA 94134, 415-467-1300. Or 719 Fleet Bank Bldg., Providence, RI 02903, 401-521-7333. Or 245 Perimeter Center Pkwy., Suite 420, Atlanta, GA 30346, 404-396-2276. Or Suite 500, 5501 LBJ Freeway, Dallas, TX 75240, 214-991-3788. Geographic processing company. GDMS software package, for use on a mainframe computer, digitizes and encodes multiple layers of geography which can be filled with tabular data.

Compucon, Inc., P.O. Box 401229, Dallas, TX 75240, 214-680-1000. Geographic processing company. Offers computer-generated maps and graphics for market analysis in communications industry.

Compusearch. 347 Bay Street, Suite 709, Toronto, Ontario, Canada M5H 2R7, 416-862-8869. General demographic/research service. On-line access to Canadian demographic data. Analyzes direct mail lists for Canadian/U.S. customers.

Compusulting Associates, Ltd., P.O. Box 418, Centerport, NY 11721, 516-261-0488. Supplies microcomputer systems for newspapers and other media.

Criterion Incorporated, 11100 Roselle Street, San Diego, CA 92121, 619-455-0162. General demographic/research service. DEMIS is a database containing 1980 census data with files on geographic boundaries, annual estimates for noncensus years, projections. Software also available for human resource analysis, including: affirmative action, site location, demographic forecasting, boundary analysis, local government planning.

Datamap, Inc., 6874 Washington Avenue South, Eden Prairie, MN 55344, 612-941-0900. Geographic processing company. Supplies maps of block groups, postal carrier routes, census tracts, zip codes, counties, other geographic configurations.

Data Resources, Inc., Consumer Research, 27 Hartwell Avenue, Lexington, MA 02173, 617-861-0165. Forecasting service company. Model of U.S. economy. Has demographic/economic model which forecasts population by household type, age, income.

Datatron Corporation, 303 Massachusetts Avenue, NE, Washington, DC 20002, 202-544-4333. Direct mail demographics company. National Information System is designed to target audiences for direct mail and telemarketing campaigns.

David Bradwell and Associates, Inc., 880 Las Gallinas Avenue, San Rafael, CA 94903, 415-479-4980. Consulting services. Consulting activities include city/county population/employment projects, industrial, commercial, residential real estate feasibility studies.

Demographic Research Company, Inc., 233 Wilshire Blvd., Santa Monica, CA 90401, 213-451-8583. Or 124 Chestnut Street, Philadelphia, PA 19106, 215-922-5225. General demographic/research service. Programs for direct response prediction. Customized demographic analysis for consumer product companies.

Donnelley Marketing Information Services, 1351 Washington Blvd., Stamford, CT 06902, 203-965-5454. General demographic/research service. American Profile database contains census data, five-year projections, plus bells and whistles including auto ownership characteristics. Produces site evaluation reports and market analyses. ZIPprofile is designed for direct mail analysis. ClusterPlus is their cluster analysis product. X/CensusPlus allows a scanning or ranking of the 1980 census.

DSR Marketing Systems, Inc., Tollway North Office Center, 108 Wilmot Road, Deerfield, IL 60015, 312-940-8200. Consulting services. Concentrates on management consulting, market research, demographic analysis for retailers.

DUAL-Comm Inc., Suite 1250, 1015 15th Street, NW, Washington, DC 20005, 202-789-8695. General demographic/research company. Processes census data. Prepares projections of client-specified populations. EEO DATA SYSTEM gives data and technical advice for affirmative action/human resources planning.

Election Data Services, Inc., 1522 K Street, NW, Suite 626, Washington, DC 20005, 202-789-2004. Specializes in using census demographics in election consulting. GeoPol, a targeting system consisting of census and voting data tied to precinct census geography.

Financial Marketing Group, Inc., 377 Park Avenue South, New York,

NY 10016, 212-685-5930. Services institutions needing demographic data to comply with regulatory requirements.

Florida Applied Demographics, P.O. Box 20071, Tallahassee, FL 32316, 904-222-6910. Consulting services. Specializes in population esti-mates/projections, socieconomic estimates, analytical population studies, small scale demographic studies.

The Futures Group, 76 Eastern Blvd., Glastonbury, CT 06033, 203-633-3501. Forecasting service company. Specializes in forecasting, plan-ning, policy analysis, competitive analysis, market studies, technol-ogy assessment. FUTURSCAN, interactive computer system allowing subscribers to forecast time series, access projections, modify fore-casts using their own data.

Geographic Data Technology, 13 Dartmouth College Highway, Lyme, NH 03768, 603-795-2183. Geographic processing company. Sells boundary files usable for computer mapping of data, calculating area, determining centroids for various levels of geography. Also sells street network files.

Geographic Systems, Inc., 100 Main Street, Reading, MA 01867, 617-942-0051. Geographic processing company. Produces computer maps for business analysis. Sells companies software to produce maps themselves.

The Glimpse Corporation, P.O. Box 1943, Alexandria, VA 22313, 703-836-6800. Puts data on microcomputer diskettes. Offers direct mar-keting services and market information services. Produces demo-graphic estimates and projections.

Infomap, 3300 Araphoe, Boulder, CO 80303, 303-444-3613. Geo-graphic processing company. Offers computerized color maps of client and census data.

International Data and Development, P.O. Box 2157, Arlington, VA 22202, 703-521-1219. Sells software for processing large databases. MOD series designed to process 1970 and 1980 census tapes.

Kellex Data Corporation, 20B Village Square, Glen Cove, NY 11542, 516-671-8520. Human resources service company. Provides availabil-ity statistics for affirmative action planning and litigation defense.

LAM Consulting, Inc., 220 Albert Street, Suite 211, East Lansing, MI 48823, 517-337-7750. Consulting services. Specializes in consulting relating to research data management.

Market Growth, Inc., 1625 I Street, NW, Suite 204, Washington, DC 20006, 202-296-2346. Consulting services. Performs custom analyses of the Hispanic community.

Market Statistics, 633 Third Avenue, New York, NY 10017, 212-986-4800. General demographic/research company. Specializes in sales and marketing analysis. Market Statistics Data Bank provides annually updated county demographics. CENTAB provides census data extracts prepackaged by zip code.

Menkin-Lucero & Associates, 1419 Broadway, Suite 215, Oakland, CA 94612, 415-452-4696. Consulting services. Specializes in small area and regional population projections.

Metromail, 901 West Bound Street, Lincoln, NE 68521, 402-475-4591. Direct mail demographics company. Has file of consumer households geocoded to census geography and matched to census information.

Modeling Systems, Inc., Ten Emerson Place, Suite 3E, Boston, MA 02114, 617-227-6778. Geographic processing company. Applies mathematical models to problems involving spacial distributions of people, firms, or activities.

MPR, Inc., Suite 550, 600 Maryland Avenue, SW, Washington, DC 20024, 202-484-9220. Supplies 1980 census data for states, counties, cities on diskettes. Also supplies statistical analysis and tabulation software for analyzing and generating reports on microcomputer.

National Decision Systems, Inc., 539 Encinitas Blvd., Encinitas, CA 92024, 619-942-7000. Or 405 Danbury Road, Wilton, CT 06897, 203-834-1360. General demographic/research company. Offers site evaluation and market analyses based on census data. Site Search identifies sites according to demographic data. ADS/AIM, analytic tools locating areas where client's customer profile dominates. ZIP CODE PLUS includes census data, current estimates, projections.

National Planning Association, 1606 New Hampshire Avenue, NW, Washington, DC 20009, 202-265-7685. Forecasting service company. Provides by subscription two annual series of projections — The National Economic Projections Series & Regional Economic Projection Series.

National Planning Data Corporation, P.O. Box 610, Ithaca NY 14851, 607-273-8208. Or 227 Fort Pitt Blvd., Pittsburgh, PA 15222, 412-471-6732. Or 14679 Midway Road, Dallas TX 75234, 214-980-0198. Or 1801 Avenue of the Stars, Los Angeles, CA 90067, 213-557-0158. General demographic/research company. Source of annual current estimates of population, households, income, age for census tracts/zip codes. MAX System offers site evaluation and trade area analysis. Labor Force Essentials provides detailed occupation data by race and sex.

Orrington Economics, Inc., P.O. Box 3756, Arlington, VA 22203, 703-527-5990. MICROMARKETS II is a demographic database on diskette, includes 1980 census data plus current estimates. Can be used on IBM and Apple microcomputers.

Personnel Research Incorporated, 1901 Chapel Hill Road, Durham, NC 27705, 919-493-7534. Human resources service company. Specializes in statistical analysis, data preparation, software support for EEO litigation and development of affirmative action plans.

Planning Data Systems, 1601 Walnut Street, Suite 1524, Philadelphia, PA 19103, 215-665-1551. Geographic processing company. Digitizes map coordinates and builds machine-readable geographic files using client data.

Psychological Services, Inc., 3450 Wilshire Blvd., Suite 1200, Los Angeles, CA 90010, 213-738-1132. Human resources service company. Offers statistical analyses of census data and personnel records for affirmative action planning and EEO litigation.

Public Demographics, Inc., 4616 N. Edgewood Avenue, Cincinnati, OH 45232, 513-681-3735. Or One Walbrooke Circle, Scarsdale, NY 10583, 914-723-2429. Applies demographic analysis to solving community problems. MARKiTS analyzes economic potential of community. INDUSTRIAL MARKiTS looks at regions assets and liabilities.

Rand McNally & Co., P.O. Box 7600, Chicago, IL 60680, 312-673-9100. Geographic processing company. RANDATA, locational database, includes population estimates for over 40,000 smaller, noncensus places as well as census data. Also offers automated cartographic files.

Resource Information Associates, P.O. Box 254, 125 N. Main, Eaton Rapids, MI 48827, 517-663-7139. Specializes in serving local and regional planning agencies wanting to use census data on microcomputers.

R.L. Polk & Co., Motor Statistical Division, 431 Howard Street, Detroit, MI 48231. Direct mail demographics company. National consumer household file consists of 73 million households, developed from merging names and addresses from sources including auto registrations and telephone directories.

Robert Hagan Associates, 3703 Riverwood Court, Alexandria, VA 22309, 703-780-7569. Consulting services. Offers statistical consulting from assessment of data needs through data acquisition and results analysis.

Robinson Associates, Inc., 15 Morris Avenue, Bryn Mawr Mall, Bryn Mawr, PA 19010, 215-527-3100. Uses census and other demographic data to prepare marketing strategy studies.

Sammamish Data Systems, 1413 177th Avenue NE, Bellevue, WA 98008, 206-644-2442. Specializes in making census data available for microcomputers. Census Data System features software and report generators for 1980 census data. Desktop Information Display System prepares full color maps based on zip codes, census tracts, counties.

Survey Sampling, Inc., 180 Post Road East, Westport, CT 06880, 203-226-7558. Specializes in drawing samples for telephone, mail, and door-to-door surveys of households or companies.

Tri-S Associates. P.O. Box 130, Ruston, LA 71270, 318-255-6710. Consulting services. Prepares customer demographic and economic reports for market research site selection, reapportionment and redistricting, long-range planning.

Urban Data Processing, Inc. 209 Middlesex Turnpike, Burlington, MA 01803, 617-273-0900. Geographic processing company. SAGE system specializes in matching addresses to geographic codes. Area Profile Report System offers demographically based site evaluation.

Urban Decision Systems, Inc., 2032 Armacost Ave., Los Angeles, CA 90025, 213-820-8931. Or 180 Post Road East, Suite 10, Westport, CT 06880, 203-226-8188. General demographic/research company. ON-SITE gives 1980 census demographics, current estimates, five-year forecast for site evaluation and market research.

Urban Science Applications, Inc., 200 Renaissance Center, Suite 1230, Detroit, MI 48243, 313-259-6933. Geographic processing company. Merges client-supplied data with other databases to graphically analyze markets.

Vistar Software, Inc., 659 W. 61st Terr., Kansas City, MO 64113, 816-361-0169. OCTAGON allows user to ask questions of census data. User must acquire census data on diskettes elsewhere.

Western Economic Research Co., 13437 Ventura Blvd., Sherman Oaks, CA 91423, 213-981-9762. Specializes in preparing moderately priced reports and maps as marketing aids for planners/administrators in California and Western states.

Wharton EFA, Inc., 3624 Market Street, Science Center, Philadelphia, PA 19104, 215-386-9000. Forecasting service company. POPMOD uses Wharton's national econometric mode to build economic and demographic forecast models.

V

Colleges & Universities Affiliated With The Certified Financial Planner (CFP) Program

COLLEGE/UNIVERSITY	CONTACT PERSON
BENTLEY COLLEGE Center for Continuing Education Bentley College Waltham, MA 02254	Steve Quigley (617) 891-2135
BROOKHAVEN COLLEGE 3939 Valley View Lane Farmers Branch, TX 75234	Rosanne Uhlarik (214) 620-4722
BROWARD COMMUNITY COLLEGE 1000 NW Coconut Creek Blvd. Pompano Beach, FL 33063	Donna K. Grady (305) 973-2205
CALIFORNIA LUTHERAN COLLEGE Thousand Oaks, CA 91360	Carol Keochekian (805) 492-2411
CALIFORNIA STATE COLLEGE SAN BERNADINO 5500 State College Parkway San Bernadino, CA 92407	Keith Johnson (714) 887-7665
CHARLES STEWART MOTT COMMUNITY COLLEGE 1401 East Court Street Flint, MI 48503	Dean E. Haley (313) 672-0200
CLEVELAND STATE UNIVERSITY 2344 Euclid Avenue Cleveland, OH 44115	Barbara Ludwig Michelle Shadrake (216) 687-2144
COLLEGE OF MOUNT SAINT VINCENT Riverdale, NY 10471	Kathleen MacDonald (212) 549-1120
DAYTONA BEACH COMMUNITY COLLEGE P.O. Box 1111 Daytona Beach, FL 32015	Dr. Janie T. Lawhorn (904) 255-8131
DRAKE UNIVERSITY College of Continuing Education 2700 University Avenue Des Moines, IA 50311	Ann L. Schodde (515) 271-2525

EASTERN WASHINGTON UNIVERSITY   Jackie Fick
216 Showalter Hall   (509) 456-4401
Cheney, Washington 99004

EMORY UNIVERSITY   Karen Hybel
School of Business Administration (404) 329-7838
Atlanta, GA 30322

FOX VALLEY TECHNICAL INSTITUTE   Dr. Ken Huddleston
1825 N. Bluemond Drive   (414) 735-5689
P.O. Box 2277
Appleton, WI 54913-2277

FRANKLIN UNIVERSITY   Peg Thoms
Division of Continuing Education (614) 224-6237 x 224
201 S. Grand Avenue
Columbus, OH 43215

GEORGE WASHINGTON UNIVERSITY   Lavona Gray
801 22nd Street NW, #T401   (202) 676-5755
Washington, DC 20002

GEORGE WASHINGTON UNIVERSITY -   Tellie Baltes
  Virginia   (804) 838-8444
Tidewater Center
2019 Cunningham Drive
Hampton, VA 23666

GOLDEN GATE UNIVERSITY   Dr. Murry Duetsch
5050 El Camino Road   (415) 961-3000
Los Altos, CA 94022

GOLDEN GATE UNIVERSITY   Gale Raymond
Mathers AFB   (916) 362-4440
Sacramento, CA

GOLDEN GATE UNIVERSITY - LA   Tony Branch
818 W. 7th Street, 10th Floor   (213) 623-6000
Los Angeles, CA 90017

GOLDEN GATE UNIVERSITY - SF   John Coyle
536 Mission Street   (415) 442-7000
San Francisco, CA 94105

WM. RAINEY HARPER COLLEGE
Algonquin & Roselle Roads
Palatine, IL 60067

Dorothy Giese
(312) 397-3000

HONOLULU COMMUNITY COLLEGE
874 Dillingham Blvd.
Honolulu, HI 96817

Walter P. S. Chun
(808) 845-9122

INDIANA UNIVERSITY
IU/PUI Division of Continuing Studies
Union Building
1300 West Michigan Street
Indianapolis, IN 46202

Casey Maas
(317) 264-4501

JERSEY CITY STATE COLLEGE
Jersey City, NJ 07305

William P McNulty
(201) 547-3001

LINDENWOOD COLLEGE
St. Charles, MO 63301

Marilyn Leach
(314) 946-6912

LOYOLA COLLEGE
4501 N. Charles Street
Baltimore, MD 21210

Patricia Farrar
(301) 323-1010

METROPOLITAN STATE COLLEGE
Dept. of Management and Finance
1006 11th Street
Denver, CO 80204

Dr. Patricia
  Duckworth
(303) 629-3181

MORNINGSIDE COLLEGE
Sioux City, IA 51106

Gary H. Koerselman
(712) 274-5118

MONMOUTH COLLEGE
West Long Branch, NJ 07764

Mario A. Taddeo
(201) 222-6600

OKLAHOMA CITY UNIVERSITY
2501 N. Blackwelder
Oklahoma City, OK 73106

Patrick W. Fitzgerald,
  Ph.D.
(405) 524-1945

PALM BEACH JUNIOR COLLEGE
4200 Congress Avenue
Lake Worth, FL 33461

William Graham
(305) 439-8010

ROOSEVELT UNIVERSITY
430 S. Michigan Avenue
Chicago, IL 60605

Barbara Tzur-Jenks
(312) 341-3637

ST. JOHN FISHER COLLEGE
3690 East Avenue
Rochester, NY 14618

Robert Holtz
(716) 586-4140

ST. VINCENT COLLEGE
Latrobe, PA 15650

Irving A. Pratt
(412) 238-7878

SAN DIEGO STATE UNIVERSITY
San Diego, CA 92182

Anne Wright
(619) 265-6255

SCOTT COMMUNITY COLLEGE
Belmont Road
Bettendorf, IA 52722

Dorothy Martin
(319) 359-7531

SHORELINE COMMUNITY COLLEGE
16101 Greenwood Avenue North
Seattle, WA 98133

Robert Hughes
(206) 546-4101

UNIVERSITY OF ALABAMA
UAB Special Studies
917 South 11th Street
Birmingham, Al 35294

Thomas W. Ash
(205) 934-3870

UNIVERSITY OF ARKANSAS at Little
   Rock
Dept. of Economics & Finance
33rd and University
Little Rock, AR 72204

Dr. Ashland Vibhakar
(501) 569-3354

UNIVERSITY OF CENTRAL FLORIDA
Department of Finance
Orlando, FL 32816

E. Theodore Veit
(305) 275-2525

UNIVERSITY OF DETROIT
651 E. Jefferson
Detroit, MI 48226

Mildred L. McGurgan
(313) 446-1168

UNIVERSITY OF HARTFORD
Division of Adult Educational Services
West Hartford, CT 06117

Dr. E. Michael Brady
(203) 243-4387

UNIVERSITY OF HOUSTON
Downtown College
1 Main Street
Houston, TX 77002

Carol Roberts
(713) 749-2061

UNIVERSITY OF MIAMI
P.O. Box 248005
Coral Gables, FL 33134

Rich Carey
(305) 441-9266

UNIVERSITY OF MINNESOTA
Extension Classes
202 Wesbrook Hall
Minneapolis, MN 55455

Phil Lundblad
(612) 373-1855

UNIVERSITY OF MISSOURI - KC
5110 Cherry
Kansas City, MO 64110

Gilda Bormaster
(816) 276-2205

UNIVERSITY OF SOUTHERN
   CALIFORNIA
Divison of Professional
   Development Programs
CES 200 University Park
Los Angeles, CA 90007

Linda Butcher
(805) 987-7857

UNIVERSITY OF SOUTHERN
   CALIFORNIA - Bay Area

Richard Lucier
(408) 379-1050

UNIVERSITY OF SOUTHERN
   CALIFORNIA - Valley
1601 Carmen Drive
Camarillo, CA 93010

Linda Butcher
(805) 987-7857

UNIVERSITY OF TAMPA/METRO
   COLLEGE
Tampa, FL 33606

Dr. James Drake
(813) 253-8861

UNIVERSITY OF TULSA
Division of Continuing Education
600 South College Avenue
Tulsa, OK 74104

Charles L. Scott
(918) 592-6000

UNIVERSITY OF VIRGINIA   Susan J. Lipton
Roanoke Regional Center   (703) 982-7922
2103 Electric Road SW
Roanoke, VA 24018

VI

Case Studies

CASE STUDY 1.   FIRST INTERSTATE & PENNINGTON BASS

You drive into Hobbs, New Mexico, on Highway 180, a newly paved four-lane, which runs clear out to Dallas through the Llano Estacado, the high flat plain that is West Texas. Grass is mostly what grows here, although it is no longer, as described by conquistador Coronado when he passed this way in the 16th century, "chest high on a man." Hobbs is the kind of place where cattle and sheep greatly outnumber the 100,000 area residents, who frequently describe their habitat as "flat, dry and ugly." Annual rainfall averages 15 inches and summer temperatures hover around 100 degrees. The town's tallest building rises a full five stories above Broadway, the main drag (US 82), and is the home of field offices for oil industry companies like Texaco, Halliburton, and Llano, Inc.

A tourist who took a wrong turn somewhere on the way from Phoenix to Abilene would see no more than just another small town in Southeastern New Mexico, and the few who knew something about financial services would surely not recognize Hobbs as the site for a progressive experiment in financial planning. But it was toward this dot on the map that veteran planner Lee Pennington aimed his chartered plane early in the summer of 1983.

Pennington was on his way, with fellow planner Bill Whorton, to a first meeting with Robert C. Quigley, president of First Interstate Bank of Lea County. Quigley, a First Interstate Veteran with branch banking experience in California and Arizona, had arrived in Hobbs in 1981 to take over the $45 billion bank holding company's local bank, a $190 million asset institution. What he found was an unsettled market whose fortunes rose and fell with the oil and gas business, and competitors who were not handling major depositors very efficiently. In fact, depositors' assets had been draining out of Hobbs' four major banks for several years, primarily to large Texas institutions which offered coordinated private banking and financial planning services for high net worth individuals. "Customer's liquid assets were spread all over the place," Quigley recalls. "Getting them to consolidate their resources was an obvious opportunity."

Shortly after settling in Hobbs, Quigley made his observations known at a regional bankers discussion group, part of a new affiliation program for community banks run by Sheshunoff & Co., the bank and thrift information company based in Austin, Texas. Before some 300 bank presidents and CEOs, Quigley suggested that small banks might offer something called "financial planning" as a means of competing in an increasingly deregulated environment, and do so perhaps through cooperative arrangements with independent, outside financial planners. Few agreed. "They were afraid of exposing their deposit base," Quigley recalls, "but it's silly to live with your head in the sand. Sophisticated investors at any bank are going to make their money work for them, so the obvious thing is to provide a service that will help them reach their goals. At the same time, you create loans and fee income from other banks' services."

Quigley's search for a qualified outsider led him to respond in late 1982, to an advertisement in *The Wall Street Journal* placed by Charles Kaczmarek, a veteran Houston planner who was then offering financial planning services to banks. Too far away to help at reasonable costs, Kaczmarek referred Quigley to Lubbock-based Pennington Bass Co. But Quigley did some research of his own before making the phone call that led to Pennington and Whorton's chartered plane ride. Out on the sparsely settled Llano Estacado, references were easy to find. Pennington Bass had done solid planning work in the past for El Paso National, one of Quigley's correspondents, and First Interstate's ad man, it turned out, had been a Pennington Bass planning client for years.

When Pennington and Whorton met with Quigley, a second meeting was arranged, and within a month Whorton was back in Hobbs, this time with Mark Bass (Pennington's partner). Together they presented the details of their 15-man firm to First Interstate's board, and shortly thereafter, as a final test, Quigley and some of his officers and board members became clients of the Lubbock firm. In keeping with the frank and open approach of its presentation, Pennington Bass made no special effort on the plans, and charged its going rate.

First Interstate's favored customers and other high net worth folks in and around Hobbs soon began receiving invitations from the bank to seminars, hosted jointly by First Interstate's trust department and Pennington Bass. Those attending learned what comprehensive financial planning was and how the bank's services fit into the process. A gratifying number became planning clients at fees of 2 percent of the prior year's income. First Interstate kept 25 percent of that, but the real income was a rise in trust business and the capture of a number of significant new customers, who switched to First Interstate after going through the planning program.

The relationship has progressed well since 1983. When it became apparent early on that bank officers didn't really understand what financial planning was, Bill Whorton and other Pennington Bass planners ran a series of seminars in Hobbs, not only to teach the process but to instruct officers throughout the bank how to identify prospective planning clients. Once they grasped the principle, the program started to snowball, and the bank moved from a seminar approach to a referral system. Today all officers receive two blank referral cards each month, which they fill out and send on to Ron Miller, who works as a planning coordinator in the trust department. Miller then calls prospects and arranges initial appointments with planners, who now spend six days or more a month in Hobbs. During gaps in their appointment schedules, Whorton and others walk downstairs and visit with officers on the bank floor, answering questions about planning and reinforcing the now strong ties between the planners and the general operations of the bank. Bank officers often sit in on client conferences to learn about counseling techniques and get an even better grasp on a methodology they have found ideal for matching customers' needs with other bank services.

In June 1985, referrals were rolling in, and 30 bank customers were somewhere in the planning process, which can take up to a year to complete. In addition, First Interstate has set up a retail center in one of its branches, and had plans to add more simplified planning service to tax preparation, consumer loans, and other bank services offered at that location. The bank and Pennington Bass are talking about training officers to deliver planning service to lower income customers, and the planning firm is helping the bank look for computer software that would allow officers to automate the screening and referral process. "Our relationship with Pennington Bass won't end," says one First Interstate vice president. "We recognize their expertise and expect to continue referring wealthier clients to them. But we have both realized that economics and logistics make some kind of bank provided service the next step."

Few other bankers running smaller community institutions will begin with the same depth of experience with planning as Bob Quigley. Long before coming to Hobbs, he had been a planning client of a

San Francisco firm and had tried, unsuccessfully, to get a group of Bay Area First Interstate branch managers to introduce the service in their banks. In short, he was a knowledgeable believer. The success of financial planning in Hobbs results almost entirely from his commitment.

CASE STUDY 2.   SETTING UP AN INTERNAL PROGRAM AT THE SAVINGS BANK OF UTICA

A more challenging bank market than metropolitan Utica, New York, would be difficult to find. Population growth is practically nil, unemployment high, and there is plenty of competition. "To grow you have to take market share," says Gary E. Gildersleeve, until recently the only CFP in the area and vice president at the $650 million Savings Bank of Utica.

Around 1980, bank management decided their institution would not survive if it continued to offer no more than the traditional transaction services. Well respected it might have remained, but the crowd of new competitors coming over the horizon was going to walk all over the bank unless it began expanding product lines and emphasizing service.

Looking for a way to make personnel comfortable with their necessarily expanded role in this scheme led to Gildersleeve's interest in financial planning and his CFP. Other bank officers are currently enrolled in the course, operated on a correspondence basis by the College for Financial Planning in Denver, and as they gain expertise these individuals will move into the bank's basic planning program for middle market customers. It got off the ground in 1984 and really got rolling the following summer. The bank had purchased a six-part planning seminar/workshop program from Bankers Systems (Box 97, St. Cloud, Minnesota 56302, 800-328-2342), one of the largest community bank service companies in the country, and was getting good attendance through a deal with the local branch of the state university system as well as through its mailings to its own customer lists.

As Gildersleeve got more deeply involved with financial planning and began to understand its value for customers in every income group, the bank began exploring ways to expand its insurance sales and introduced seminars on pre-retirement planning and funding college education. "Planning came first and other things started to fall into place," says Gildersleeve.

The Savings Bank of Utica for a long time had been able to sell savings bank life insurance (SBLI) in a maximum amount of $30,000. In 1983, they hooked up with American Life Insurance Co. to take advantage of a new provision of New York banking law which allows banks to enter areas of investment opportunity provided they risk less than 10 percent of their capital. Now, Savings Bank customers can buy insurance in any dollar amount, the first $30,000 as an SBLI policy and the rest as an American policy. More recently the Utica bank negotiated a deal with American General to sell that company's universal life and single premium tax-deferred annuities. In mid-1985, another arrangement with Phoenix General to sell homeowners insurance was pending state regulatory approval.

The seminars are sold at breakeven rates ($35 to $40 per couple for each financial planning unit) or given away to attract new business. More fee income is generated when seminar attendees or bank customers decide to buy one or more of the 16 modules in the Bankers Systems computerized planning program. This process begins with the customer filling out a questionnaire, oftentimes assisted by a financial planning officer who charges a small fee for his or her time. Then the data is sent off to Bankers Systems headquarters in St. Cloud, Minnesota, and a printed report comes back in a few days. Officers review this document, then go over it with customers. The report earns another fee, and better yet, most planning clients wind up buying bank products and services, which produces even more income. For other products and services not offered by the bank, planning officers make referrals to well-qualified sources in the community. Eventually, says Gildersleeve, the bank may become a true one-stop shop by signing up to work with Bankers Systems' broker dealer, a subsidiary of Mutual Benefit Life, and has prepared to sell mutual funds and other securities by hiring a properly licensed employee. There are also plans afoot to add in-house planning support, especially for more complex cases. Gildersleeve and other planners have been looking at personal computer planning software for this purpose. Planners already run illustrations for insurance products.

Inside the bank's organization, the planning program sits atop a three-tiered customer service division. Floor offices refer to customer account specialists and they refer in turn to financial planning officers. All members of management and all employees have gone through the planning workshops, and many actively sell the planning workshops and reports. Moving from the limited subject seminars to a full financial planning program, Gildersleeve believes, has helped the bank break out of its older customer base and begin attracting business from younger, middle-class residents of the Utica area. It's also substantially increased sales of nontraditional bank products.

CASE STUDY 3. STATE BANK OF MEDFORD, WISCONSIN — INNOVATIVE BANK-BASED FINANCIAL PLANNING

The State Bank of Medford in Medford, Wisconsin, is a $90 million asset community institution serving a rural community of 4,500 midway between Green Bay and Minneapolis. Despite its lack of huge resource, the bank has constructed one of the more innovative bank-based financial planning efforts in the country. It has done so with almost no reliance on outside services.

The bank basically dismantled its glass-walled loan department, located behind the teller area in the lobby, and replaced it with a Financial Planning Center, decorated in subdued tones and hardwood paneling. The Center ties together five bank services that were formerly separate: personal financial planning, new accounts, discount brokerage, trust, and investment products and management. In 1985, the bank spent about $2 per capita to promote its new one-stop nature in the surrounding community.

President Ronald Issacson went with financial planning as a defensive measure. For several years before inception of the Center in 1984, the outflow of deposits had been increasing, as customers responded to a flood of literature from other financial services companies. Stockbrokers, insurance agents, gold and silver specialists, even neighboring lending institutions that offered alternative investments had begun soliciting and winning business from Issacson's customers.

The Center didn't happen overnight, however. In fact, Issacson and his management team spent months looking at alternative financial planning configurations before settling on the current concept. Turnkey financial center packages, they felt, were either too expensive for a small bank to justify or simply not what the bank was looking for. Setting up financial planning as a subunit of the trust department or a standalone service was also considered and rejected. Issacson did not want to add yet another layer to the bank's already highly segmented structure. He was also careful to avoid saddling financial planning with an image of being only for the old and rich. The very idea of working with outside financial planners seemed unnecessarily risky because Issacson believed they could quite possibly become yet another group of pirates and spirit away even more of the bank's declining number of customers. He finally settled on the internal Center concept, which creates plenty of cross-selling opportunities.

The Medford bank program is not entirely self created. Discount brokerage is offered through Bankers Discount Brokerage Service, which Issacson likes because it only accepts orders from client banks. Trust specialists, paid on an hourly basis, are imported one day a week from a larger community bank far enough away not to be a direct competitor.

The bank did buy a financial planning software package for $2,500 from IFDS of Atlanta, one of the leading companies in the field. The software is run on an IBM PC to produce plans priced from $150 to $300, depending on their complexity. About the only services not available from the bank in mid-1985 was tax preparation, but Issacson had plans to build a protecting wall here, too, probably by hiring a CPA.

Mark J. Rieland, vice president of marketing, sums up the reason for the Medford bank's bold approach. "There is a whole new breed of customer and a whole new set of competitors," he says. "The customer is better educated, more informed. There are more opportunities for the customer and they are going to take advantage of those opportunities. Banks have to handle these things that middle income and upscale people want or they are going to go someplace else. We need the skills of financial planning so we can tell them about these various investments. We have to be honest and up front or we're going to lose deposits. Customers will want to consolidate their deposits and in certain situations will move all of them out to where they are getting their financial planning. We want them to do it through us."

When looking at the future, Issacson sees the soundness of his bank linked to flexibility that comes from offering financial planning. He encourages other smaller banks to get into the business, or at least to make sure they have someone on staff who can answer customers' questions about planning strategies and investments.

CASE STUDY 4.   SUCCESSFUL BANK/ FINANCIAL PLANNING FIRM JOINT VENTURES: MISSOURI SAVINGS-P&W LTD.

One of the more successful joint venture examples we have come across is at the St. Louis-based Missouri Savings Association, a $700 million thrift, which teamed up with P&W Ltd., a local planning firm, in the summer of 1984. Officers at the Association had known P&W's president, Paul Weisman for years, so they had little trouble working out the details of a new company called Missouri Savings Financial Services.

The joint venture agreement specifies a 50-50 split on ownership and profits after commission to the five planners employed by P&W who man desks in two of the thrift's 15 branches doing plans ($60, $30 for IRA customers) and selling annuities, life insurance, and investment products like mutual funds. The agreement also contains a buy-out clause that allows either party to purchase the other's interest. Both Weisman and Missouri Savings insisted on it. The joint venture is managed by a six-person committee, three from the thrift and three from P&W. Among its other functions the committee discusses all investment products before they're sold to customers.

Perhaps the most interesting aspect of the program is the client asset-tracking system, based on software written by Weisman's son, who works at P&W. Once a customer has signed on as a client, all his or her funds (both inside and outside the bank) are tracked. Just getting its hands on this total customer information, never previously available, has helped the thrift target its marketing effort.

But, more significantly, after several months the data showed conclusively that customers were moving assets into the thrift and that the program was attracting many new customers who used various thrift services more than the historically average new customer.

"We're finding that people are actually saving more with us," says John Young, senior vice president. "There was, of course, an initial concern that there'd be an outflow of funds, but we concluded that if a person was really interested in a type of savings product we didn't offer, they'd leave us anyway." In its first three months, the joint venture signed up 120 customers for financial evaluations and investment suggestions, with 92 percent of client funds for investment coming from outside the Association.

Since the outset, the joint venture has paid all its expenses, for secretarial work, computer time, and a point-system bonus for employees of the thrift who are rewarded for referrals. Missouri Savings has largely handled marketing, promoting the planning service through statement stuffers and print advertising in major local newspapers. But P&W offers periodic planning seminars and helped produce planning videotapes which are played in branch lobbies. The joint venture has also paid for a brochure which describes financial planning services for business customers.

CASE STUDY 5.   LARRY CARROLL and THE BANK OF HARTSVILLE, SOUTH CAROLINA: A LIVING PARTNERSHIP

When Larry Carroll, a Charlotte, North Carolina-based planner, and Joe Cothran, president of the $50 million Bank of Hartsville, South Carolina, struck a handshake agreement early in 1984, neither man anticipated problems. Carroll liked his prospects in the area served by the bank, which includes several major employers and an above average percentage of affluent residents. Cothran had checked on Carroll with friends at NCNB, and was satisfied he was dealing with the best financial planner in the area. But beyond settling on a series of seminars to introduce planning service to bank customers and other well-to-do Hartsville residents, the pair discussed little marketing strategy. "We went in with the understanding we were running blind and would modify as needed," says Carroll.

In March 1984, 135 invitations from the bank produced a better than 25 percent response, and Carroll returned to Hartsville to face a full house for his first presentation: a 30-minute introduction of the bank-linked service. "I was really disappointed," recalls Cothran. "Larry emphasized the fee too much, and the whole thing was too hardsell and divorced from the bank."

Immediately afterwards the pair had a frank discussion. "Misunderstanding caused the problem," says Carroll. "I thought I was supposed to introduce the service, but Joe had sent out invitations that led people to believe they would be listening to planning ideas." Satisfied that the next time around would be different, Cothran soon sent out a second set of invitations. To help Carroll prepare Cothran sent evaluations filled out by attendees of the first seminar on to him.

The next month, in front of a more homogeneous group of 40, "Carroll was fantastic," says Cothran. The audience apparently agreed. Sign-ups for planning service, priced at $900 to $3,000, were heavy over the next few weeks.

For the third seminar in May, fresh invitations coaxed back some of the folks dissatisfied by the first presentation. Carroll shone again. "Evaluate the sign-up rate in terms of family buying units," Carroll points out, "and we achieved about a 25 percent conversion ration."

Obviously, that result would not have been achieved without Cothran's commitment and Carroll's flexibility. Indeed, a less entrepreneurial banker who did not believe in the power of financial planning — as a business builder and a competitive tool — might well have stopped the experiment after the first disastrous episode.

CASE STUDY 6.   COMPETITION FROM THE BIG EIGHT ACCOUNTING FIRMS

A few of the "Big Eight" accounting firms have been in the planning business in their own way for the better part of a decade. Both

Coopers & Lybrand and Touche Ross have well-developed programs which span the market from customized services for high net worth individuals and corporate executives to seminars for middle class groups and rank and file employees. Touche planners have even produced several editions of a well-thought-out planning handbook that has sold well in bookstores across the country. Ernst & Whinney also has a well-established, nationally coordinated program. But four other members of the Big Eight (Price Waterhouse, Deloitte, Peat Marwick, and Arthur Young) are in the throes of developing their practices and Arthur Andersen, the largest of them all, seems content to limit its planning practice to a few select offices. Indeed, after a flurry of activity over the past several years and promises to dominate the market, most Big Eight firms have substantially reined in their financial planning departments and are proceeding cautiously with a wary eye on the SEC and Congress.

The advantages for these firms of being in the planning business are obvious. Providing one more service to executives of audit clients helps cement relationships. Providing it to executives of competitors' clients may act as a foot in the door should they decide to change auditors or look for tax advice or management consulting. The existence of this type of practice helps attract qualified personnel, and it is one more marketing advantage when competing with smaller firms for the business of small business.

Like large institutions in any field these major firms are unwilling to risk their good names and the bulk of their business in order to pursue an as yet unproven market, especially in uncertain times. In addition to increased prospects for new regulation of their traditional businesses as a result of recent Congressional hearings (most particularly those held by the Dingell Committee), major firms fear they may be forced to register under the 1940 Investment Advisors Act if they continue to offer financial planning. As the Act is currently interpreted, CPAs are exempt as long as their investment advice is "incidental to" the traditional activities of the profession, but it is becoming clear that the SEC does not consider that financial planning falls into that category. Registration under the 1940 Act is a distinctly unpalatable alternative for major firms. Not only would they face significant logistical problems in compliance, but their internal finances would become a matter of public record and the SEC would acquire almost plenary access to their books and records in connection with periodic audits.

The Big Eight, by and large, believe they can avoid registration by limiting planning service to existing clients and imposing strict quality controls to prevent partners and managers from doling out the type of investment advice which would bring them under the Act. But this course may place them at a significant disadvantage in competing for planning business against other CPAs and the rest of the financial services companies crowding into the field. Major firms may claim they can provide investment advice to planning clients through outside consultants or by working with clients' existing advisors, but many observers believe that the market wants total advisory service, including investment advice, from one source.

As if this complication weren't enough, it also seems that as large accounting firms expand their planning practices they will run into vexatious internal problems. For example, it is certainly conceivable that audit partners, who have been informally advising executives of client companies for years, may well get miffed when tax department planners take over their roles, especially if the new advisors propose markedly different strategies. Though national planning coordinators may downplay the risk, there is always the possibility that corporate clients will go elsewhere for big ticket audit, tax, and consulting work because financial planning advice for decision maker executives didn't work out. Last but not least, serious conflicts of interest are apt to occur. "What do you do," muses Don Wright, partner in charge of Arthur Andersen's Executive Financial Planning Service, "when you have negative inside information because you're the auditor of a company whose stock your planning client wants to buy? We can advise conceptually and quantify the pros and cons of investments, but specific recommendations are out."

CASE STUDY 7.   COMPETITION FROM SMALLER NATIONAL AND LARGER REGIONAL ACCOUNTING FIRMS

This group, which runs the gamut from outfits like Laventhol & Horwath and KMG Main Hurdman, which have annual revenues over $200 million to 100-200-person firms like Mayer Hoffman Mc-

Cann (Kansas City) and Kraft Brothers, Esttman, Patton & Harrell (Nashville) which dominate local markets, poses a much stronger competitive challenge in financial planning than the Big Eight. Younger, faster growing and more aggressive, these smaller firms are less hobbled by internal conflicts and more likely to view financial planning as an opportunity to solidify client relationships.

McGladrey, Hendrickson & Pullen, an eastern regional firm, has spent the past two years establishing a planning section in each of its offices. Prior to its merger with Fox & Co., Alexander Grant had a four-office pilot project underway. In early 1985, Laventhol was gearing up a program aimed primarily at executives. Last spring, Seidman & Seidman, long known for its expertise in tax matters, merged with the Boston firm of Bornhofft & Co., at least in part to acquire the expertise of that firm's fee-only planning subsidiary, Bornhofft Financial Services. But perhaps the most striking effort of all among the larger firms in this group is taking place at KMG Main Hurdman, the nation's ninth largest CPA firm and the U.S. component of the world's fourth largest.

Between 1983 and 1985, John Mullen, KMG's national coordinator of personal financial planning, and Mike Dunleavy, director of new product development, led a multi-million-dollar crash program to create training courses, find and modify computer software, educate the firm's 3500 U.S. employees about financial planning so they would be able to market the new service, and work out a string of joint ventures with banks and other financial services companies. From out of nowhere, the firm has emerged as a major player in the industry, with somewhere between 12% and 15% of its U.S. employees manning one of the largest planning groups in the country.

Such thoroughgoing change would probably have been impossible at a Big Eight firm, if only because their mammoth domestic operations, built on SEC audit business, have developed political enertia. But KMG's client base is largely small companies. Eighty per cent of them post under $100 million sales and far and away the majority fall in the $5 million to $30 million range, just the type of outfits whose entrepreneurial owners make prime planning clients.

Dunleavy discovered this soon enough in early 1983 when he responded to a directive from Frank Gaffney, national director of tax services, to find out about financial planning. Partners had been calling in from the field with questions, and Gaffney wanted to know what the firm was doing. Dunleavy's survey turned up a few of the firm's 85 offices, like Minneapolis and Los Angeles, with active planning practices, but he also learned that KMG had no consistent approach to providing the service. Talking with independent planners and others in the business, the new products director came to understand that planning is a personally oriented, full-scale service. Unfortunately, though, the firm's partners were not providing it. What they were doing instead, Dunleavy says, was churning out bulky written reports, an overkill response of little benefit to clients.

And yet in planning, its popularity growing daily, lay obvious opportunity. Dunleavy's market research showed that KMG was well positioned to grab a big share of the $75,000 and up income market. "Below the $50,000 level most people deal with one financial services company, and that's a bank," he says. "Between $50,000 and $75,000 they start using brokers, but many are dissatisfied with a sales-based relationship, and unless the broker is good he or she starts losing credibility with his or her customers when they begin having significant disposable income. Somewhere between $75,000 and $100,000 people start believing they need more help, and they either hire a tax adviser, or if their bank has a good private banking operation they may use that."

Dunleavy also saw the market changing. An increasing number of conscientious independent planners as well as planning efforts mounted by large financial services competitors were picking off clients in the $40,000 to $75,000 group, and because of the strong relationship inherent to the planning process, these people weren't as likely to move to CPAs as their income grew, even for one shot services. If KMG was going to keep new clients coming in the door, Dunleavy realized, the firm would have to move quickly.

What happened next has become a fairly common pattern in the development of financial planning at large financial services companies. KMG first established its high overhead, top of the market service, and then began quantitative market research to identify common concerns of lower income groups. In 1985, this knowledge was being incorporated into new computer programs, and Dunleavy predicts that by 1987 the firm will be profitably providing planning to anyone with more than a $25,000 income.

Perhaps even more significant from a competitive standpoint are KMG's joint ventures with banks and other financial services companies. Early on in the development of planning at KMG, at least two major brokerage firms knocked on the door with offers of joint ventures, and insurance companies called as well. But senior partners, well aware that their main marketing strength lay in a solid reputation for objectivity, rebuffed these offers after exploratory talks showed that the outsiders wanted to control investment recommendations, a condition no serious accountant could accept.

Not long afterwards, however, KMG worked out what has become a model joint venture with Chemical Bank, in which the firm provides complex planning at reduced rates to individuals attracted to Chemical's retail financial planning program. As a result of this experience, KMG learned how to help a bank or other financial services firm set up, introduce, and deliver planning. Due to the success of the Chemical program and increasing competitive pressures, many of KMG's former suitors have come back for a second look, and this time they're much more willing to accept the firm's insistence on objectivity.

As we have previously noted, executives in all types of financial services companies are realizing that financial planning is most easily sold if the provider has or develops a reputation for objectivity and trustworthiness. By joining with public accountants, who consistently score highest in public opinion surveys, KMG's joint ventures have added marketing clout and leapfrogged competitors with less potent reputations. In return, KMG gets access to a massive group of potential clients.

Clearly, however, it doesn't have to be KMG. Should a bank decide to go the joint venture route, there are plenty of accountants to choose from. Most likely there will soon be many more. The failure of the profession's leadership as yet to lay out ground rules may have acted as a drag so far, but CPAs providing planning is a natural development and a logical evolution of their technical skills. And besides, as accountants rapidly discover once they begin offering the service, planning is an easy sale. "We have encountered very little resistance," reports Michael Azorsky, a partner at Mayer Hoffman McCann in Kansas City, which began offering planning several years ago.

Bibliography

Albert, Andrew. "Financial Planning Shapes Up As Crucial Arena, Study Says," *American Banker*, January 17, 1985, p. 1 ff.

Anthes, William I. "Financial Planning Service Arena Has Bankers In Quandary," *American Banker*, April 11, 1983, p. 14 ff.

Barnewall, Marilyn MacGruder. "Three Sides of Financial Planning Show Up Difficulties," *American Banker*, September 27, 1983, p. 61 ff.

———. "Why Banks Have the Edge In Financial Planning Services," *Bank Marketing*, November 1983, p. 29 ff.

——— and Jerome R. Corsi. *A Banker's Pragmatic Approach to the Upscale*. The MacGruder Agency, Denver, Colorado, 1982.

Davidson, John R., "Bow Ties and Trust Departments: Micros and Financial Planning," *Vermont Bankers Association General Bulletin*, January/February 1985, p. 6 ff.

"Education Guides Financial Planning Decision," *ABA Bankers News Weekly*, July 24, 1984, p. 4 ff.

Feuchtwanger, J. Bud. "Attract Customers and Generate Fee Income With Securities-Based Products." *The Magazine of Bank Administration*, February 1985, p. 68 ff.

"Financial Planners — How to Find the Right One," *Changing Times*, December 1983, p. 28 ff.

"Financial Planning Aid May Strengthen Customer Bond: Tools May Include Books, Computer, Seminars," *Savings Institutions*, July 1983, p. 111 ff.

"Financial Planning Featured," *Illinois Banker*, November 16, 1984, p. 3.

"Financial Planning May Not Pay Yet, But Banks Are Urged to Become Players," *American Banker*, December 20, 1984, p. 24 ff.

Gross, Laura. "Prudential-Bache, in Strategy Switch, to Stress Total Financial Planning," *American Banker*, February 11, 1983, p. 3.

Guy, John W. "Financial Planning Services," *Hoosier Banker*, November 1984.

Haugh, James W. "Keogh Plans Expand Tax and Financial Planning Opportunities," *The Magazine of Bank Administration*, December 1984, p. 14 ff.

Hunter, John Jr. "Financial Counseling, Vendors: Ammunition Against Nonbanks," *American Banker*, December 7, 1983, p. 4.

Hyman, Joan Prevete. "Financial Counseling Helps Position Vermont National Against Nonbanks," *Bank Systems & Equipment*, December 1983, p. 115.

Isgur, David. "Banks Respond Slowly As Demand For Financial Planning Services Grows," *The Commercial Record,*" December 21, 1984, p. 1 ff.

Kurucza, Robert M. "Financial Planners and Banks: Potential Partners in a Growing Industry," *Financial Strategies & Concepts,* Winter 1985, p. 1/ ff.

La Tour, Jac. "Much More Than Giving Advice: Financial Counseling," *Credit Union Marketing,* Winter 1983, p. 9.

Lauterbach, Jeffrey R. "Banking on Planning," *Financial Planning,* November 1984, p. 115 ff.

———. "Small Banks of the Future," *Financial Planning,* October 1984, p. 124 ff.

———. "Testing The Waters," *Financial Planning,* March 1985, p. 162 ff.

———. "Timidly Into The Breach," *Financial Planning,* March 1985, p. 9 ff.

Madsen, Craig. "Financial Planning — Sophisticated Marketing Tool," *Trust Management Update,* June 1983.

Mandell, Lewis. "Financial Self-Portraits: A Cost-Effective Way to Reach the Affluent Market," *Bank Marketing,* March 1983, p. 9 ff.

———. "What Are the Qualities of a Good Financial Planner? *American Banker,* October 12, 1983, p. 4.

Market Facts, Inc., *The Market for Bank and Thrift Personal Financial Counseling,* Chicago, 1984.

"Moving In: Financial Planning Support For Banks," *Financial Planning,* March 1985, p. 23 ff.

"NASAA Sees Need for Uniform Regulations for Financial Planning," *Financial Services Week,* March 18, 1985.

"News Briefs," *Hoosier Banker,* March 1985, p. 4.

"Ohio Bank's Financial Planning Joint Venture Attracts Upscale Clients," *Financial Services Week,* April 1, 1985, p. 4 ff.

Olafson, John A. "The Money Manager: A 'Far-Out' Success," *Bank Marketing,* August 1983, p. 20.

Reeck, Darrell and Joan Bavaria. "Financial Services: Industry in Transition," *Insight,* November 1984.

Richards, Pierre E. "Personal Financial Planning: A New Market May Hold Profit For Smaller Banks," *Trusts & Estates,* November 1983, p. 56 ff.

Seglin, Jeffrey L. "Choosing the Right Financial Planner," *Personal Investing*, January 16, 1985, p. 5 ff.

———. "The Producer's Revolution," *Financial Planning*, October 1984, p. 66 ff.

Shanahan, James B. "Defining the Market/Packaging the Product," Banking Law Institute, March 25-26, 1985, New York.

Siegal, Sherry. "Hanging Out a Financial Planning Shingle: More Brokers Are Entering The Promising New Field of Financial Planning. Is it Worth the Effort?" *Institutional Investor*, September 1983, p. 215 ff.

Smyth, Sam. "Pricing and Cost Approaches to Financial Planning," (Unpublished speech.)

Stolz, Richard. "A Few Less Closed Doors," *Financial Planning*, March 1985, p. 156 f.

Veres, Robert. "The Best and the Brightest," *Financial Planning*, August 1984, p. 105 ff.

Waggoner, John. "Financing Small Real Estate Limited Partnerships," *Bankers Lending Letter: Lending to Small and Middle Market Companies*, June 1985, p. 1 ff.

———. "Status Go (CIGNA)," *Financial Planning*, February 1985, p. 116 ff.

White, Dr. Phllip D. "Financial Planning," The ABA National Trust and Financial Services Conference, January 28, 1985, New York.

Williams, David C. "Personal Financial Planning and Banking: A Planner's Viewpoint," ABA Trust and Financial Services Conference, January 28, 1985, New York.

Index

Affiliate, definition of, 80–81
AICPA. *See* American Institute of
    Certified Public Accountants
American Bankers Insurance
    Corporation, 91
American Express, 56
American Institute of Certified Public
    Accountants (AICPA), 49, 50
American National Bank (California),
    90, 91
American National Bank of Austin,
    Texas, 82
American Security Bank, 57
Applied Experts Systems, 33
Asset Management Group, 56
Ayco, 56
Banc One (Columbus, OH), 90
Bank holding companies, 80–81
Bank Holding Company Act of 1956,
    71, 94
Bank of America, 59, 90, 91
Bank of California, 97, 98
Bank ownership by nonbank
    companies, 70
Bankers Systems, Inc., 31, 100
Banking Affiliates Act of 1982, 80, 85,
    94, 105

Bank of Boston, 32, 58
Banks, as providers of financial
    planning, 6–8, 14–20
*Board of Governors of Federal Reserve
    System vs Investment Company
    Institute*, 73, 75, 81, 97
Boston Five Cents Savings Bank, 97
Breakeven price, 24
Broker-dealers, liabilities of, 123–127
Brokers, 51–54, 137–145
Brown vs Schleier, 90
"Bullet" approach to service, 25
Butterfield Savings and Loan (Santa
    Anna, CA), 99
Cali Computer Systems, 32
Case studies, 177–193
Certified Financial Planner (CFP)
    program in colleges and
    universities, 169–176
Certified Public Accountants (CPAs),
    48–51
Certified Public Accountants (CPAs),
    management advisory services
    of, 50
Chase Manhattan, 58
Chemical Bank, 11, 12, 15, 16, 18–19,
    20, 57, 60, 60–61, 91

CIGNA, 47
CIGNA Individual Financial Services, 58
Citibank, 97, 98
COAP, 32
College for Financial Planning, 34
  CPA enrollments in, 49
Competition, 20–21
  from brokers, 51
  from CPAs, 48–51
  and credibility, 40
  increase in, 46–47
  from independent planners, 54–56
  from insurance companies, 47–48
  from major banks, 56–64
Comptroller of the Currency, 69, 79, 82–83, 91–93, 96–97, 98, 99
Computer Language Research Corporation, 32–33
Computers, 32, 51–52
Confidence in supplier, 52, 57
Confidentiality, 6, 36
Connecticut Bank & Trust, 60, 97
Consumer Financial Institute, 32
Continental Illinois, 58, 63
Correspondent banks offering discount brokerage services to other banks, 147–157
Costs, 24, 33
Covered transaction, definition of, 81
CPAs. See Certified Public Accountants
Credibility, 40
Cross-selling, 40
Customers
  age of, 12, 16
  education of, 12
  family size of, 12
  income of, 11, 12, 17
  occupation of, 12
Dean Witter, 51
Depository Institutions Act of 1982, 80, 85, 94, 105
Deregulation, 20–21
Discount brokerages, 6–7
Discount brokers offering services to banks, 137–145

Employment Retirement Income Security Act (ERISA), 107
EQUITEC, 32, 69–70
Farmers Savings Bank (California), 99
FASTTAX, 33, 49
Federal Deposit Insurance Corporation (FDIC), 69, 78, 83–84, 95, 99
Federal Home Loan Bank Board (FHLBB), 69, 79, 85–86
Federal Reserve Act, 72
Federal Reserve Board, 69, 78, 79, 81, 88, 91, 94, 96, 99
Federal Reserve system, 72, 74
Federal Savings and Loan Insurance Company (FSLIC), 69
Federal savings banks, 85–87
Federated Investors, 32
Fees, 21–25
  and "special compensation," 109–110
FHLBB. See Federal Home Loan Bank Board
Fidelity, 32
Financial planners, 5–6
  commitment of, 6
  independent, 54–56
  qualifications of, 5–6
Financial Planners Equity Corporation, 53
Financial planning. See also specific topics
  and bank operations, 6–8, 14–20, 29–30
  definition of, 3
  expansion of, 45–46
  by insurance agents, 94
  legal boundaries of, 69–70
  process of, 3–5
  providers of, 22–23
  steps in, 3–5
  in strategic plans of banks, 21
Financial Service Corporation, 53
First American Federal, 86
First Chicago, 58–59
First Interstate, 12, 56, 57
First Interstate Bancorp, 90, 91

First National Bank of Maryland,
    United States vs, 77
First Nationwide Savings, 57
Flexibility, 7
Form ADV, 110–111, 112, 115
    filing of to satisfy state regulations,
    116
Form ADV-S, 111, 112
Form BD, 122
Fortune Federal, 86
FSLIC. *See* Federal Savings and Loan
    Insurance Company
Garn-St. Germain Depository
    Institutions Act of 1982, 80, 85,
    94, 105
Glass-Steagall Act of 1933, 70, 71–76,
    83–85, 88, 96, 97
    and joint ventures, 81
    legal precedent and, 75–76
Great American Savings and Loan
    (San Diego), 99
Gus Blass Co., State vs, 91
H.T. Hackney Company vs *Robert E.*
    Lee Hotel, 91
H&R Block, 89
Hay Group, 56
Holding companies, 71, 73
Home Owners' Loan Act, 85
Hub Financial Services, 36
Huggins Financial Services, 56
Hutton, E.F., 51
IAFP. *See* International Association
    for Financial Planning
Idaho First National Bank, United
    States vs, 77
Implementation of financial plans,
    regulations regarding, 77–78
Individual Retirement Accounts
    (IRAs), 6, 7, 97, 98
In-house programs. *See* Internal
    programs
Insurance
    credit life, 94
    property, 94
Insurance companies, 47–48
    competition from, 47–48
    joint ventures with, 48, 94–95

Integrated Resources, 53, 60
Integrated Resources Equity
    Corporation, 89
Internal programs, 31–35
    regulatory considerations, 76–79,
    107
International Association for
    Financial Planning (IAFP), 3,
    46, 49, 108, 124
    Code of Professional Ethics, 126
    CPAs in, 49
INVEST Corporation, 86–87, 89
Investment Advisers Act of 1940, 70–
    71, 79, 82, 89, 93, 107, 108–116,
    116, 124, 125
Investment advisors
    recordkeeping requirements of,
    111–116
    registration of, 109–110
    SEC definition of, 108–109
Investment Advisors International,
    58
Investment Company Institute, 97
Investment Company Institute vs
    Camp, 71–72, 96, 97
IRAs. *See* Individual Retirement
    Accounts
John Hancock Life, 90
Joint ventures, 24
    division of fees in, 89
    between Federal Reserve member
        banks and outside vendors, 88
    with insurance companies, 48, 94–
    95
    with INVEST Corporation, 86–87
    with non-member banks, 83–85
    with nonbanking subsidiary of a
        bank holding company, 80
    with outside planning firms, 35–41
    between savings and loans and
        service corporations, 85–87
Keogh plans, 6, 7, 97
Liberty National Life, 90
Limited partnerships, 98–103
McNeil, Robert A. Corporation, 99
Mandell Institute, 32
Manufacturers Hanover, 57

Manufacturers Hanover Corporation, 88
Manufacturers Hanover Money Market Corporation, 88
Market
    measurement of, 14
    "middle," 11
    receptivity of for banks to offer financial services, 14–20
    segmentation of, 11–14
Market research firms, 159–168
Marketing, 7
Merrill Lynch, 51
Money market accounts, 6
MPACT Brokers, 82
MPACT Corporation, 86
MPACT Services Corporation, 82
Mutual funds, 97
NASD. *See* National Association of Securities Dealers
National Association of Securities Dealers (NASD), 53–54, 107
    required membership in, 123
National Equity Securities Corporation, 100–101
Nationwide Insurance, 90
NBD Corporation, 59
NCNB, 57, 62
Needs oriented selling, 51–52
Networking arrangements, 79
New York Stock Exchange (NYSE), 51–53
Non-member banks, 83–85
Personal financial planning software, 131–136
Philadelphia National Bank, United States vs, 77
Planned Management Company, 103
Poughkeepsie Savings Bank, 86
Practitioners Publishing Company, 49
Preliminary decisions, 30–31
Preston State Bank, 38
Private Bank, 56
Private Financial Counseling Group, 39, 61
Prudential-Bache, 52

Quissett Corporation, 32, 33, 58, 62
Reasonable care, 125–127
Registration of bank as broker-dealer, 121–123
Regulation, 69
Regulation Y, 78
Regulatory agencies, 69
Rental agreements with outside vendors, 89–93
    drawbacks of, 93
    financial planners, 93
    insurance, 89–90
    legal precedents for, 90–91
    percentage arrangements, state regulation of, 95
    percentage arrangements, 90, 91, 94–95
    securities dealers, 93
Rhode Island Hospital Trust, 103
RIHT Financial, 56
Robert A. McNeil Corporation, 99
Roe, Martin and Neiman, 103
SAFECO, 90
Savings and loan associations, 85–87
Saxon vs *Georgia Association of Independent Insurance Agents*, 90–91
Sears, 52
SEC. *See* Securities and Exchange Commission
Securities Industry Association vs *Federal Reserve Board*, 96
Securities Act of 1933, 107, 124
Securities and Exchange Commission (SEC), 49, 69, 71, 74, 79, 82–83, 89, 96, 99–101, 107, 108–116
    registration requirements, 121–123
Securities and Exchange Commission vs *Capital Gains Research Bureau, Inc.*, 125
Securities and Exchange Commission vs *United Benefit Life*, 96
Securities Exchange Act of 1934, 79, 107, 121–122, 124

Securities Investor Protection
    Corporation (SIPC), 123
Securities regulations, 105–127. *See
    also* specific legislation
  legal foundations, 107–108
Security Pacific National Bank, 60,
    81–82
  discount brokerage services of, 81–
    82
Security Properties, Inc., 99
Services, types of, 21–25
Setting up a financial planning
    department, 27–41
  cost of, 33
  support services for, 31–33
Sexton vs *Swords S.S. Line, Inc.*, 77
"Shingle theory," 123
Slay vs *Burnett Trust*, 77
Society Corporation, 58
Software, 30, 32–33, 131–136
Spoor Behrins Campbell & Young, 56
SRI International, 46. *See also*
    Stanford Research Institute
Staffing problems, 34

Stanford Research Institute (SRI), 15,
    17. *See also* SRI International
State regulations, 116–121
Stock brokers. *See* Brokers
Strategic planning, 21
Suburban Bancorp, 57
Success, indicators of, 29–30
"10% of 20% Rule," 14
*Third National Bank in Nashville,
    United States* vs, 77
Trustee compensation, 77
Turn-key vendors, 79, 87, 89
Uniform Partnership Act, 91
United Banks of Colorado, 58
United States vs. *See* defendant
U.S. Bancorp, 57
Variable annuity contracts, 96–97
Wagner vs *Buttles*, 91
Wells Fargo, 61–62, 97, 98
Williams vs *Barton*, 77
Wingert vs *First National Bank*, 90
Wirtz vs *First National Bank & Trust
    Company*, 90
Wright vs *Trotta*, 91